Praise for *The Modern Dads Handbook*

"Fathers today are facing a whole new set of challenges in our relationships with our children, our partners, balancing work and family commitments. Most of us need help in sorting it all out. John Badalament has given us a deeply insightful and marvelously practical resource to begin this process."
—JACKSON KATZ, author of *The Macho Paradox, Why Some Men Hurt Women and How All Men Can Help* and creator of the documentary video *Tough Guise: Violence, the Media and the Crisis in Masculinity*

"In my work as a counselor over the past 25 years, it has been easy to see the impact of father absence -- physically and emotionally -- on the lives of their children. In my role as a father of two young boys it has been humbling to come to terms with my own absence, and a challenge not to deny it. John Badalament's book is more than a wake-up call for fathers like me; it is precisely the type of support I need to show up for my children and to remain present in all the ways that are so vitally necessary -- for them, for our family, and for me."
—DR. MICHAEL J. NAKKULA, father, hockey coach, Assistant Professor Harvard Graduate School of Education, coauthor of *Understanding Youth: Adolescent Development for Educators*

"Through the entrepreneurial approach of framing a vision statement, as well as assessing and integrating what has been learned from their own fathers, this workbook enables men to tackle the challenge of fatherhood in a clear, effective way. Every wife will want her husband to read this book."
—TAMARA MONOSOFF, CEO of Mom Inventors, Inc, author of *The Mom Inventors Handbook* and *Secrets of Millionaire Moms*, and a columnist for Entrepreneur.com

"With this handbook, John Badalament has given Modern Dads a Mapquest™ to family harmony. But like any directions, it's not enough to just read them. You have to get in the car and drive. Inspired by years of work with real families, including his own, these exercises will absolutely take you to a place of greater paternal integrity, trust and love."
—HAJI SHEARER, Director of the Fatherhood Initiative, Mass. Children's Trust Fund

The Modern Dads Handbook

John Badalament

The Modern Dads Handbook

by John Badalament

Published by Cole Valley Mill

The Modern Dads Handbook

by John Badalament

Published by Cole Valley Mill

Disclaimer
The Modern Dads Handbook is not a substitute for medical, psychiatric, or psychological advice or other counseling. If you have specific concerns or problems, please consult your health care provider or other appropriate professionals.

Book design by John Aldrich, john.aldrich@mac.com

ISBN 13: 978-0-615-14614-0

Visit www.johnbadalament.com
for more information about
The Modern Dads™ Newsletter,
speaking engagements, films
and other resources.

Acknowledgements

I would like to thank the following people for their inspiration, generosity, time, belief, and support along the way:

John Aldrich, Terry Real, Jonah Matranga, Haji Schearer, Jim Sullivan, Mike Nakkula, Jackson Katz, Tamara Monosoff, Juan Carlos Arean, Lonna Davis, bell hooks, Craig Norberg-Bohm, Arthur Lipkin, Susan Brady, Brewster Ely, Diane and David Jensen, Peter Badalament, Kelli Birtwell, Daniel Jensen, Carla Young, Korki Aldrich, Caroline Blackwell, Monica Sullivan, John Scully and my incredible wife Katie and two wonderful children Stella and Jake for their endless love and support through this entire process.

This Handbook is dedicated

to the memory of my father Tony Badalament – the storm

to my mother Diane Jensen – the safe harbor

to my brother Peter Badalament – the captain of our little ship

to my stepfather David Jensen – the break wall

and to my wife Katie and children Stella and Jake – the road home

Contents:

Getting Started

Introduction

Over the last five years I've spoken to thousands of fathers across the country and abroad, and I've researched, written and made a documentary film about what it means to be a Modern Dad.™ It has become very clear to me, as a practitioner and a dad myself, that for most men fatherhood today is as challenging as it is rewarding. As women have moved into the workforce, many dads – some by choice, others by necessity – have begun to be more active at home. No longer able to rely on the traditional roles of "man the breadwinner/woman the caretaker," Modern Dads have both the responsibility and the opportunity to redefine fatherhood for generations to come.

Whether it means leaving work early to make a game or a play, staying up late with a sick child, talking through a relationship problem with a partner, or attending a parent-teacher conference at school, many Modern Dads are determined to show up for our families in ways our own fathers could not or did not. However, we're also just discovering what most mothers have known for years: doing it all isn't easy. It's especially difficult when you don't have many role models to follow.

The Modern Dads Handbook walks you through *Four Practices* that will help you navigate the everyday challenges and pressures of family life. It will also equip you with practical skills and activities to stay connected, both with your children and with your partner. Whether you are married or single, co-habitating or co-parenting, a stepfather or a live-away dad, *The Modern Dads Handbook* is written for all fathers with children of all ages. Depending on your situation, you may use the Handbook in different ways.

For example:

- **For dads with newborns, infants or toddlers**
  The Handbook will help you craft a vision for the kind of relationship you want with your child, as well as develop a foundation of relationship skills and habits.

- **For dads with school-aged children**
  The Handbook will help you keep the lines of communication open and your relationship strong as your children's interests, personalities, and priorities change.

- **For dads with teenagers and young adults**
  The Handbook will help you stay close without being intrusive, talk about critical issues, and chart a new course for your relationship as your child moves towards adulthood.

Modern fatherhood is all about embracing change, having vision, and taking action. Women have traveled a great distance on the road from home to the world of work. They are not turning around. Now is the time for us as dads to ask more of ourselves. Being a father is not something you *are*, it's something you *do*. By showing up for our children and partners, learning new skills, building support networks, and measuring success by the quality and health of our relationships, Modern Dads have begun the journey on the road that leads back home. As you make your way toward this new vision of fatherhood, *The Modern Dads Handbook* will serve as your map and your guide.

How to use this Handbook

This Handbook is written specifically for dads who may not have the time or interest in reading a lengthy book on fatherhood, but want skills and information to put to use right away. I intentionally kept the writing short and to the point. The majority of the Handbook consists of what I call "actions," practical skill-building activities to do by yourself, with your children, and with your partner or close friend. These activities are sequenced to build upon each other. Viewed as a whole, the Handbook presents a complete and clear vision for modern fatherhood.

I encourage you to write in this book. You also may want to have a notebook or journal on hand in case you need more room. When finished, you will have a snapshot or portrait of your experience of fatherhood at this particular point in your life. This Handbook is truly a living document, something you may choose to pass on to your children as part of your legacy.

How the Handbook is organized

The Handbook is broken up into four main Practices. Each Practice has three Reflections. Each Reflection has one to seven Actions.

PRACTICE								
REFLECTION I			REFLECTION II			REFLECTION III		
ACTION	ACTION	ACTION	ACTION	ACTION	ACTION	ACTION	ACTION	ACTION

PRACTICES

These are the big ideas, the guiding themes for the Modern Dad.

> First Practice - Creating Your Legacy
> Second Practice - Showing Up Physically
> Third Practice - Connecting Emotionally
> Fourth Practice - Modeling Healthy Relationships

It is recommended you do the Practices in order, as they are sequenced to build upon each other. For example, the First Practice lays the foundation for the other three Practices by prompting you to explore your own family legacies. Armed with a clear sense of the past and a vision for the future, the Second Practice is about showing up both at home and at your child's school. Without awareness of physical presence, it's difficult to focus on the Third Practice: Connecting Emotionally. Finally, the Fourth Practice shifts emphasis to your adult relationships.

REFLECTIONS
These are short essays to get you thinking about a specific theme or issue. They are mostly informative, often contain research and examples, and define key terms. For instance, Reflection III of the Third Practice asks you to reflect on how well you communicate with your child, then cites research on why it's important and explains two essential ways to improve communication.

ACTIONS
The Handbook is designed to encourage informed action. Actions vary widely, from writing a letter to your father to taking a quiz about the details of your child's life to learning how to manage anger. Some Actions focus on building particular skills; others may have you do an activity with your child.

Suggestions for Using *The Modern Dads Handbook*
There is no 'right way' to use this book. While I have suggested that you do the Practices in order, you may want to start with a certain action that seems most relevant now. Or you may jump from Practice to Practice in no particular order. Whether you tackle all the Practices or focus just on what's most important to you, consider:

Taking your time. There is no need to rush through the Handbook. Give yourself time to think about an idea or to prepare yourself for one of the actions. Pay attention to your reactions to the material.

Setting a schedule for yourself. It may be helpful to devote a consistent time during your day or week. Whether that means getting up an hour early one or two days during the week or taking a lunch time to use the Handbook, scheduling a regular time will give you consistency.

Doing the Handbook with a friend or a group of dads. Doing the Handbook with others is a good way to build a community of dads, discuss the content, and keep you accountable for your progress.

How this Handbook came to be

In my educational consulting work, I do an activity with students where they anonymously write down two questions they've always wanted to ask their father. No matter what the cultural, socioeconomic or ethnic background of the students, the most common two questions are almost always the same: "What was his relationship like with his father?" and "What was his childhood like?" Though they may not ask, children want and need their father's stories, even if they never knew who their father was. I call it the elephant in the living room of child development: the missing stories of men's lives, particularly men's emotional lives.

Somehow, at the age of twenty-five, I knew that if I was ever going to be a dad myself, I had to face my own father. The following is a short excerpt from an article I wrote about our relationship:

I walked into my father's office to settle a score; he thought we were going out for lunch. For the twenty-five years prior to that day, nobody in our family had found the courage to speak honestly and directly with my father. All that would change in just ten short minutes.

I told my father that we weren't actually going to lunch, that he should stay seated and not respond to anything he was about to hear. He had been given plenty of time to speak over the years; this time was mine. Barely able to breathe, I said, "You've done a lot of great things for me as a dad." After describing a few, such as how he supported my love of baseball and patiently taught me how to drive, I said, "And... I want you to know that growing up with you was also very difficult. You were irresponsible, alcoholic and abusive. As a consequence, I have struggled with self-worth for most of my life."

He opened his mouth to speak and for the first time in my life, I raised my hand and without a word, motioned for him to stay

*silent. I knew that if I allowed him to deny, explain or minimize
what I was saying, like most loyal sons, I would back down from
speaking my truth...*

Confronting my father at the age of twenty-five was the single
most difficult, emotionally vulnerable moment of my life. As a
white youth of European-American descent, I was taught that
vulnerability got you nothing but trouble, and thus learned to
hate it. The currency of my suburban boyhood was as follows:
being tough, "getting" the girls and holding your own in sports
competition. If you had no currency, you were at risk of verbal or
physical reprisals. At all costs, I avoided situations where I could
be taken advantage of, proved wrong or look like a 'whimp' or
a 'pussy.' Implicitly, discussing feelings and relationships with or
around other boys was forbidden.

When I confronted my father that day, I assumed it would mark
the end of our relationship, that he would want nothing more to
do with me. Paradoxically, in making myself vulnerable before
him, we actually grew closer. While we didn't necessarily spend
more time together, speak more often or agree on everything,
a more open and honest dialogue developed between us. We
became more like two adults than a father and a child. The effect
of that one conversation was deep and long-lasting.

Two years ago my father became ill from years of neglecting his
diabetes. As his condition worsened, it became clear he wouldn't
be leaving the hospital. I remember looking him in the eye one
afternoon and saying, "You can go now. There's nothing left to do
here." He looked back at me, smiled, teared up and nodded. Our
peace was made. A few days later he quietly passed away.

Personally and professionally, as an educator and counselor, I have seen the tremendous impact fathers have on their children, whether present or absent. In an effort to raise awareness and spark dialogue about this subject, I created a documentary film, *All Men Are Sons: Exploring the Legacy of Fatherhood.* The film follows the lives of five men from diverse backgrounds as each explores his father's legacy; it initially aired on PBS in 2002. Since then, I have been lecturing about fatherhood to parent groups in schools, community organizations, therapists, corrections facilities, and others across the country.

The initial response to the lectures surprised me. I was warned not to expect many dads to show up, that the crowd would be mostly women. Wrong. Men have consistently outnumbered women at most of my lectures. And not only did dads show up - they engaged in substantive discussions.

While there were differences in how men experienced fatherhood, two universal themes emerged in my lectures. First, men want an outlet or a forum to discuss their lives as fathers and as men, but rarely seek one out. Secondly, despite having a *desire* to build healthy relationships with their kids and/or partners, dads often feel like they lack the necessary skills to do so.

Inspired by these conversations and themes, I created *Dialogues With Dad,* a workshop (and retreat) bringing fathers and sons, and fathers and daughters, together to strengthen their relationships. The concept was simple: get fathers and children in the same room, share stories about important topics, teach them how to talk and listen to each other skillfully, and coach them on how to keep the connection going. The results were extraordinary.

A ten-year-old boy used one of the activities on "speaking assertively" to let his dad know how much his yelling frightened him. The dad, floored by his son's feedback, made an agreement to get it under control. After a father-daughter workshop, a group of young girls said they'd "never seen men talk like that," referring to the stories dads told about their own boyhood. Consistently, fathers and children left *Dialogues With Dad* feeling closer, better able to handle conflict and more equipped to have heart-to-heart talks on a regular basis. For most, *Dialogues With Dad* was a much-needed tune-up; for some, it was the grease to keep their already solid relationship rolling; and for a few, it was a new beginning altogether.

After speaking and leading workshops for the past five years, the next question seemed obvious: could I write a handbook that would combine the *practicality* from *Dialogues With Dad* with *the information and spirited discussion* from my lectures? Could a book capture the energy of a roomful of dads, provide key research in a digestible format and teach usable skills? The answer, I hope, is yes.

The Four Practices

The First Practice
Creating Your Legacy

In The First Practice, you'll have the opportunity to think about the quality of relationship you're trying to develop with your children, the attitudes and behaviors you hope they will emulate and the legacy you wish to pass on. I always like to balance idealistic thinking with reality; you will also be asked to consider what skills, knowledge, and support you may need to realize your vision for the future.

As we look forward, we must also look back. In one of the opening lines of my documentary film, *All Men Are Sons: Exploring the Legacy of Fatherhood*, therapist and author Terry Real says, "Each man is a bridge. He spans the father that came before him and the children that will come after him... and his life is literally the distance between those two points." Beyond genetic coding, we as dads can largely determine what does and does not come across that bridge.

The First Practice prompts you to explore your own relationship with your father (and mother), whether he was present or absent. By sorting through the gifts he's given you and the liabilities he's left you with, you will gain a clearer understanding of how to create a positive, hopeful legacy for the next generation.

By sorting through the gifts he's given you and the liabilities he's left you with, you will gain a clearer understanding of how to create a positive, hopeful legacy for the next generation.

An important last step in The First Practice involves having a heart-to-heart with your dad, regardless of his presence or absence in your life. This conversation, done through letter writing, is essential to bridging the past, present and future generations. You may choose to express gratitude, tell him how much he meant or means to you, say things you've never said but always wanted to, hold him accountable for his bad behavior or let him know he's been forgiven.

Reflection I

The Dad's Vision Statement

Imagine 20 years from now your child is approached to be in a documentary film about fathers. Now, imagine the filmmaker asks your child to describe his/her relationship with you. What do you hope your child would say? What do you hope your child would NOT say?

Whether you're a builder, banker, entrepreneur, or musician, a key ingredient to success at work is having clarity about your mission or vision. Who are you? What do you do? What do you want? Where are you headed? As the saying goes, 'If you stand for nothing, you fall for anything.' Fatherhood is no different.

Without a vision, it's easy to get into the habit of being more reactive and less proactive. Take the example of the dad who wanted good, open communication with his children. In his Dad's Vision Statement he listed the important issues (drugs and alcohol, peer pressure, sex and dating, etc.) to talk about with his children at different ages. Unlike the dad who finds himself discussing the topic of alcohol on the morning after his son comes home drunk for the first time, the dad with a Dad's Vision Statement would have already laid the groundwork for dealing with this situation.

Similarly, it's easy to become more passive without a clear sense of vision. Take, for example, the dad who allowed his wife to do the bulk of the limit-setting with their young children. As he thought through the big picture, he realized that being passive while they were young could result in his never really connecting with his children. By creating a Dad's Vision Statement he became motivated to start sharing the load when it came to setting limits and generally being a presence in their lives.

Being an active, involved dad is as much about ongoing anticipation and preparation as it is about showing up at your child's games or helping with homework. Creating a Dad's Vision Statement and then revisiting it periodically is an essential step in active fatherhood.

It's important to recognize that doing a Dad's Vision Statement doesn't mean you should try to mold your children into the people *you think they should be.* To the contrary, you should consistently pay close attention to who they are becoming, find ways to support their uniqueness and keep your own expectations in check. The Dad's Vision Statement helps you stay on top of your own need for self-growth as your children mature.

By the time you reach the end of *The Modern Dads Handbook,* you should revisit your Dad's Vision Statement to see if anything has changed.

ACTION #1
Prepare to Write Your Dad's Vision Statement

Imagine 20 years from now your child is approached to be in a documentary film about fathers. Now, imagine the filmmaker asks your child to describe his/her relationship with you. With this in mind, respond to the questions below:

1.
Describe 5 things you hope your child would say to the filmmaker about his/her relationship with you.
Examples may include: "I hope my child would say she felt like I really valued her opinion even if I didn't agree with it," or "I hope my child would say that he learned respect for women by watching me."

1 _____
_____

2 _____
_____

3 _____
_____

4 _____
_____

5 _____
_____

2.
Describe 5 things you hope your child would NOT say about his/her relationship with you.
Examples may include, "I hope my child would not say that our relationship was one of image and not substance. My dad did all the right things but I never felt connected with him," or "I hope my child would not say that I was a terrible listener."

1 _____

_____

2 _____

_____

3 _____

_____

4 _____

_____

5 _____

_____

ACTION #2
Write Your Dad's Vision Statement

Your Dad's Vision Statement will guide you in developing the kind of relationship you want with your child. It will help you make important choices and set forth your priorities in your relationship. Please do the following:

Reflect on your responses to Action #1. Then, choose 2 from each list (what you hope they say and don't say) that are the most important/challenging for you and fill in the box to the right.

EXAMPLE:

1. I hope my child says...

   "My dad always paid attention to me."

   What I am doing today....

   I try to pay attention to what she's doing at school. I make one-on-one time for her at home.

   What I will do....

   I will continue to make time for her every day. Also, I will make sure to stay aware of her changing interests.

2. I hope my child does *not* say....

   "He was too hard on me."

   What I need to stop doing...

   I need to stop worrying about his lack of interest in sports. I need to stop putting so much pressure on him.

   What I will do more of...

   I will encourage him to follow *his* interests. I will talk with him about the pressure my dad put on me to be a star athlete.

I hope my child says...

What I am doing today...

What I will do...

I hope my child does NOT say....

What I need to STOP doing...

What I will do MORE of...

ACTION #3
Fulfill Your Dad's Vision Statement

What skills, knowledge and support do you need to be the father that you want to be for your family? If you have trouble, ask your partner or someone you trust what they think.

SKILLS:

_____

_____

_____

_____

KNOWLEDGE:

_____

_____

_____

_____

SUPPORT:

_____

_____

_____

_____

ACTION #4
Find a Witness

In order to have some accountability and support in realizing your Dad's Vision Statement, it's important to have a witness. Find someone close to you (another dad, a friend, your partner, etc.) with whom you would feel comfortable discussing your Dad's Vision Statement.

WHO:
I plan to talk to

WHEN:
I will talk to them

Reflection II

Looking Back at Your Father's Legacy
(whether he was present or absent)

Inside of us, we carry our father's legacy. This may include his values, habits, attitudes, stories, or, at the very least, his genetics. Thus, one of the central tasks for every man - even those whose fathers were absent - is to get as clear as possible about how that legacy may affect him as a parent... for better and for worse.

Each generation of dads has a responsibility and obligation to turn and face the past with an honest and loving eye. The love is mainly about our children; exploring the past is a way of saying, "I care enough about you to pass on the gifts I've been given and to protect you from whatever harm has been done to me." Similarly, by looking back, we can acknowledge our gratitude for the good our father, and those before him, have done. We can bring them peace.

We cannot, however, protect our children from the mistakes of the past if we are not honest about how our father's mistakes or shortcomings: a) affected us as young boys; b) still affect us today as men; and c) may have become liabilities to us as fathers.

For many men, this process of exploring their father's legacy may bring up powerful feelings of anger, sadness, disappointment and grief. Whichever of those painful feelings we refuse to face will likely get passed on to our children. I could not, for example, hope to stop the legacy of rage that has run through my family if I did not face the painful feelings of what it was like witnessing my father's angry outbursts.

A *liability* is defined as the likelihood or probability of something happening; anything for which somebody is responsible, especially a debt; something that holds somebody back.

Think of your father's mistakes as liabilities to manage for the next generation.

As the saying goes, "Pass it back or pass it on."

ACTION #1
Identify the Gifts and Liabilities From Your Father

It is imperative that we come to view our fathers (even if absent) realistically, not in black and white terms. If we overly idealize them, we may miss the liabilities we carry. If we degrade them, refuse to see anything positive (even the gift of our life), we may end up holding resentment and never move into forgiveness.

By seeing our fathers as flawed human beings who did the best with what they had, we remain humble as fathers ourselves. Then, we can help our own children to see us realistically - not as heroes or as villains - by owning up to our mistakes and striving to do better.

To the right is a partial list of Gifts your father may have given you and Liabilities he may have left you with. Circle as many as apply to your relationship with your father. Feel free to add any Gifts or Liabilities that are not on the list, but apply to you.

GIFTS

A good work ethic

Instilled sense of security/family

Faced down adversity

Warm, caring, loving

Kept in touch consistently

Showed humility

Assertiveness

Showed up to events

Shared family stories

Empathy

Handled conflict responsibly

An active and involved parent

Respected women as equals

A good listener

Expressed individuality and passion

Self-assured and confident

Valued diversity

Treated others kindly

Spirituality

Involved in community life

LIABILITIES

Often or completely absent

Didn't control anger

Deceptive

Overly critical

Couldn't tolerate vulnerability

Avoided conflict

Wouldn't talk about feelings

Workaholic

Addiction to alcohol/drugs

Unwilling to ask for help

Uninvolved in daily parenting

Kept up appearances

Rarely showed up at events

Sexist attitudes towards women

Blamed others for his problems

Lacked self-confidence

Cast a big shadow

Disrespectful to others

Didn't stand up for himself

No consequences for his actions

ACTION #2
Bridge The Past and Present

Choose 3 Gifts from the list in Action #1 that you want to pass on to your children and fill in the chart below. For example, if your father's gift was that he showed up at all of your games/events, you may be trying to pass this on by rearranging your schedule at work. You will know you're successful by asking your child if they think you show up enough.

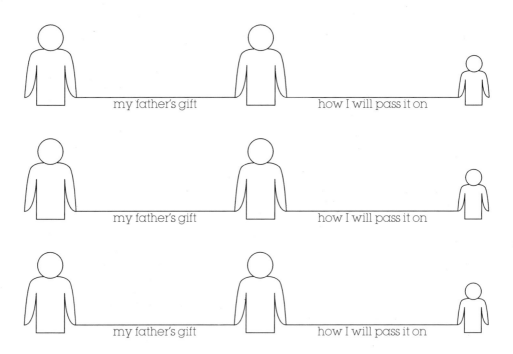

my father's gift   how I will pass it on

my father's gift   how I will pass it on

my father's gift   how I will pass it on

Now, choose 3 Liabilities from the list that you're determined not to repeat and fill in the chart below. For example, your father's emotional absence or lack of warmth left you feeling distant as a boy. Today, you may struggle to connect emotionally with your children. You could do differently than your father by reading "Emotional Intelligence" by Daniel Goleman and talking with other dads about how they connect with their children.

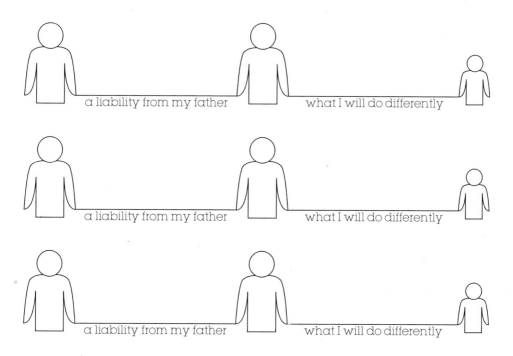

a liability from my father   what I will do differently

a liability from my father   what I will do differently

a liability from my father   what I will do differently

ACTION #3
Explore Your Mother's Legacy

A man's relationship with his mother affects how he will parent his own children. Take a moment to answer the following questions.

1. What gifts did your mother give you that you intend to pass on to your children?

2. What are the liabilities she has left you with? How are you protecting your children from repeating her mistakes?

3. Ways she interacted with your father that were healthy and positive:

4. Ways she interacted with your father that were unhealthy or upsetting to you:

5. What messages did she give you about men in general?

6. Ways she treated you that made you feel good:

7. Ways she treated you that made you feel bad
    or uncomfortable:

8. How the women in your life have been similar to and/or
    different from your mother:

ACTION #4
Examine the *Cultural Circles of Influence* on Your Fathering

Where did you learn to be a father? What does it mean to be a 'good' father? How should a father handle authority and discipline? Are there ways a father should and should not act? As you think about the father you want to be, it's important to examine the many cultural influences (past and present) that shape your beliefs about fatherhood. Choose all the 'cultural circles of influence' below that you most identify with. In each circle write an example of how your fathering has been influenced. Feel free to add any cultural influences not listed.

CULTURAL CIRCLES OF INFLUENCE

Ethnicity

Family Structure

Religion

Race

Orientation

Social Class

Economic Status

Language

Country/Nation

Education

Region/Neighborhood

Example:

Ethnicity

I make sure to hug my children and show them I love them. In Latino culture most fathers are very affectionate with their children.

Example:

Education

My dad went to college, I was expected to as well. Education is very important to me as a dad.

ACTION #5
Find a Witness

Understanding the many different ways our parents' legacies affect us is not always easy. Sometimes those connections are clear, for example when we catch ourselves saying something exactly like our father did; other times we may be blinded to how our father's legacy affects us today. In order to gain more insight about these connections, as well as communicate your intentions to repeat/do differently than your parents, please do the following:

Find someone close to you (another dad, a friend, your partner, etc.) and discuss your responses to Actions 1 to 4.

NOTES/THOUGHTS:

_____

_____

_____

_____

_____

_____

_____

_____

_____

_____

_____

_____

_____

Reflection III

Having A Heart-to-Heart With Your Dad

(even if he has passed on or isn't in your life)

In this last section you will be asked to 'have a talk' with your father through letter writing. *This process is equally important whether your father has passed on, is no longer in your life, or you have an active, ongoing relationship with him.* Having a heart-to-heart talk with your own father is important for three reasons:

1) *It allows you to acknowledge your gratitude for the important role he's played in your life.*

2) *It gives you the opportunity to hold him accountable for the mistakes he's made and move towards forgiveness.*

3) *It paves the way for developing an open, honest dialogue and deeper connection with your own children.*

Letting your father know how thankful you are is among the greatest gifts a son can give. What father would not want to hear about the positive legacy he's passed on to his children? Whether you thank him for the sacrifices he's made, the qualities he's instilled, or simply the life he's given you, each man has this gift to give his father… even if he was never there.

Holding your father accountable for his mistakes is also a gift you can give. When I described to my father the ways his anger damaged me as a boy, and how I still struggled with his legacy as a man, he didn't know what to say. Yet, three crucial things happened as a result of that exchange. First, he later apologized for hurting our family – something he may not have done if I didn't hold him accountable. Secondly, I gained self-respect by having the courage to be honest with him. Finally, when he died years later, it was peaceful; he no longer carried guilt for his mistakes. He left knowing that nothing was unspoken between us and that he had been forgiven.

There is a difference between accountability and blame. For example, the responsibility for how I handle my father's legacy belongs to me no matter how great his mistakes. I alone must fill the empty spaces and cool the rage left by my father. Holding him accountable, letting him know the damage he did, paved a way to forgiveness; blame would have made forgiveness impossible.

Forgiveness or making peace is essential to creating a hopeful legacy for your children. If you want your children to be open and honest with you, you must have the courage to do the same with your own father, either literally or spiritually.

Note: This same activity can be done for your relationship with your mother.

ACTION #1
Write Three Letters to Your Dad*

Write the following three letters in order. The exercise is a way to have 'the talk' with your father between your own two ears. You may decide to send or read these letters to your father; you may not. You may instead decide to read them to a friend or partner. This activity is more about the *process* of writing the letters. What you do with them is up to you.

Note: If you find yourself resisting this activity or are having difficulty writing anything negative about your father, it may be due to one of the following reasons:

- You feel disloyal, selfish or mean writing about your father's negative behaviors. Remember, every parent makes mistakes, including you. It is the job of each generation to look back, acknowledge the mistakes, show gratitude for the gifts, and try to do better with their own children. Acknowledging the mistakes does not mean your father didn't try his best. You can celebrate the positive and be honest about the negative at the same time.

- You feel like you're complaining or being self-pitying. There is a big difference between self-pity and self-empathy. Imagine this scenario: First, try to recall your father's negative behaviors when you were young. For example, maybe he was overly critical or didn't show up to important events. Now, imagine doing those same behaviors to your children. How would they feel if you didn't show up or constantly criticized them? Terrible, right? Finally, try to show the same empathy you have with your own children for the 'little boy' part of yourself. Just as they would feel terrible, you probably did too.

*The idea for these three letters was created by Belinda Berman, LCSW.

1

Write to your father about what it was like for you growing up with (or without) him. Describe what was positive, as well as what was difficult or negative. Think about the things you've wanted to say to him, but never have. You may cover your entire childhood or choose to focus on a particular time period or even a specific incident.

2

Write FROM YOUR FATHER'S PERSPECTIVE (the letter should start with 'Dear Son,'). This letter should capture what you IMAGINE your father would say to you in response to letter #1. How would your father react to that letter? Would he accept your point of view? Would he argue certain things? Would he be loving, hurt or angry? Imagine, as best you can, his response.

3

Write again FROM YOUR FATHER'S PERSPECTIVE. This letter should capture what you HOPE or WISH your father's response would be. In other words, if he were to respond in the best possible way to reading letter #1, what would he say? This letter is a way for you to imagine your father giving you everything you wished he would have.

The First Practice: Creating Your Legacy

End of Practice Commitments

Based on what you've learned in The First Practice, consider making 2 to 3 commitments to yourself, your children or any other important people in your life. Write in as little or as much detail as necessary:

1

2

3

The Second Practice
Showing Up Physically

In today's world, finding time to show up for our children can be incredibly difficult. Many dads spend long hours at work, leave early, get home late, or spend long periods on the road traveling. Add to that picture a separation, a second family, or a child with a busy schedule of activities and finding time gets even harder.

The phrase 'quality time' was initially used in the 1970's as a way for parents to 'have it all;' to work hard and stay connected at home. The idea was that doing something 'meaningful' or 'of quality' could replace lost hours with a child. There are two problems with this concept. First, what is 'meaningful' to a dad may not be 'meaningful' to his child. Secondly, the expectation of 'quality' adds a burdensome pressure on children, especially when the dad lives away or rarely sees the child.

A healthier definition of quality time is: being fully present (not somewhere else in your mind or on the cell phone), doing something you both want to be doing, and not worrying about the outcome of the experience. Using this definition as a guide is less convenient - we can't schedule quality time - and asks more of us as dads.

Finding time to show up for your children at home or at school can be incredibly difficult. Yet being present is the cornerstone to building a close relationship.

Spending *quantity* time is no less important. Sociologist Michael Kimmel says, "It's quantity time - hard hours of thankless, unnoticed drudge work - that creates the foundation of intimacy."[1]

Children also need time to just simply hang out with their dads, whether running errands, driving to school, or fixing things. It doesn't all have to be fun or meaningful. The more time you spend with your children, the more in-tune with each other you become. If you are a live-away dad or have very limited contact with your children, remember that your children also need time to "just be" with you. Though you may feel pressure to make the most of your time together, try *not* to plan too many activities or make it *all* about fun.

Reflection I

The Importance of Ritual Dad Time

One great way to make sure you're spending quality time with your child regularly is to create a Ritual Dad Time. This is different than your daily family rituals you may already do, like sharing meals, walking to school, reading together, etc. Rather, this is special, once per month, one-on-one time with dad. Think of it as the father-child equivalent of a couple's 'date-night.' This can be started at any time, with children of any age (newborn to adult). My daughter and I, for example, started 'daddy-daughter breakfast' when she was ten months old.

The purpose is to build in time for you and your child to foster your bond: share stories, transmit your values, discuss important issues, or just enjoy each other's company in a non-pressured way. Beyond whatever you *do* during the Ritual Dad Time, the true and lasting value comes from keeping your commitment to show up for these special hours with your child on a regular basis.

Guidelines for Ritual Dad Time:

1. ***Get together as father/child at least once per month.*** *Minimally for at least 1 - 2 hours and with only one child at a time (this may be difficult for larger families, but essential for building a one-on-one relationship).*

2. ***Choose an activity you both agree on.*** *You may allow your child to choose or alternate who decides. I don't recommend executive decisions, except in cases of extreme resistance (more on that below).*

3. **Make sure you talk during your time together.** *Going to a movie or a game is fine. Using what William Pollack (author of* Real Boys*) calls "Action Talk" (i.e. shooting baskets or playing video games while talking) is great, but as men we also need to model face-to-face dialogue for children of all ages. We don't always need a distraction! Every 3-4 months, use your Ritual Dad Time to do The Relationship Inventory (see Third Practice).*

4. **Be consistent.** *The ritual does not have to be on the same day each month, but make sure it happens so your child can count on it. I suggest scheduling your next ritual time at the end of each time together.*

Examples include: Going for a meal, taking a walk, visiting another town, going for a bike-ride, cooking a meal from a foreign country, working on a building/fix-it project, taking a drive, going to a sporting event, playing a game, doing an art project, etc.

For live-away dads: Depending on how often you see your child, your ritual may either be done less frequently (every 3, 6 or 12 months) or you could do a long-distance ritual, such as a monthly letter or on-going project.

For dads with infants or newborns: Think about visiting different environments that may stimulate your child's different senses, such as a park with a lot of birds, the beach, a crowded playground, a quiet forest, live or recorded music, etc.

ACTION #1
Create Your Ritual Dad Time

Make 'the pitch' to your child and expect some resistance. Express that you would like to try this once per month for six months. My suggestion is to make this a request on your part, something YOU are asking of your child. For example, a father I know told his 11th grade daughter that he wanted to have time with her before she goes to college; on the face of it, she would be doing this for him. Also, make it clear that you have no other agenda than to have fun and spend time doing things they want to do on a regular basis; call it a bribe or just a nice offer.

If met with total resistance, I advocate making it mandatory. That's right, mandatory. The resentment and resistance will almost certainly fade. I once prescribed this ritual time for a father and teenage son who were constantly in conflict with each other. Part of their problem was that they had too few positive experiences together. Younger kids will be far less likely to resist.

Finally, it's important to let your child's mother know what you're doing up front. This will reduce the likelihood of her having any resistance. Explain what you're doing and why this ritual time is so important. Also, listen and take her concerns seriously. On the positive side, she may offer some good suggestions or tips as well. Keep your child's mother in the loop.

Brainstorm some possible rituals:

_____

_____

_____

_____

_____

_____

_____

ACTION #2
Keep a Log of Your Ritual Dad Time

You can use the space provided in the Handbook or use your own journal. The idea is to reflect on the experience each time, if only briefly. Think about what went well, things you discussed, what didn't go well, etc. Plan on doing your ritual for at least 6 consecutive months.

If after the first or second month your ritual time is not going well, consider the following:

- Are you giving your child a choice about how the time is spent?

- Are you totally present during your time together (not talking on the cell phone, not stopping to run errands, not having the TV on)?

- Talk with your child's mother or a friend about what is happening and ask for their suggestions.

- Talk with your child about ideas for what you could do to improve your time together.

Since *you* are initiating the ritual it's important to first look at your own behavior and see what you could change.

FIRST MONTH

What We Did:

My Reflections:

Next Ritual Time
(what/when):

SECOND MONTH

What We Did:

My Reflections:

Next Ritual Time
(what/when):

THIRD MONTH

What We Did:

My Reflections:

Next Ritual Time
(what/when):

FOURTH MONTH

What We Did:

My Reflections:

Next Ritual Time
(what/when):

FIFTH MONTH

What We Did:

My Reflections:

Next Ritual Time
(what/when):

SIXTH MONTH

What We Did:

My Reflections:

Next Ritual Time
(what/when):

Reflection II

Being a Presence at Home

To my own father, home was a place to rest or recharge. He came and went as he pleased, spending most of his time working or socializing. Beyond breadwinning, the majority of the day-to-day parenting - setting limits, communicating with school, nurturing, cooking, etc. - was left to my mother. His lack of involvement was not atypical for dads of his generation.

As a Modern Dad, I am expected and want to be more of a presence than my own father. Being a presence means getting involved in the 'everydayness' of family life at home (no matter what your family structure is), from consistently setting limits to helping with homework to putting away the dishes. It means doing what sociologist Arlie Hochschild called *The Second Shift*, a term used to describe the second job most working women are left to do when they come home at night - housework and childcare.[2] Modern Dads who do *The Second Shift* teach their sons and daughters an expanded view of gender roles. Men don't simply 'help out' or 'opt out' - they are full participants in all aspects of home life. Recent research done by John Gottman found that when men did more domestic labor, their partners were more attracted to them.[3]

Dads who are not a presence - because they let their child's mother (or partner) do everything, prefer to be 'fun dad' or simply ignore responsibilities - are what's been referred to as TPFA dads (Technically Present, but Functionally Absent). For example, my dad was mostly a TPFA dad even though we only saw him on the weekends after my parents divorced. His desire to have fun, be liked, and to be our 'buddy' seemed to be most important. He did little in the way of setting limits or providing consistency.

Given how radically gender roles have shifted in the last generation, most Modern Dads have a bit of the TPFA dad in us. A good way to prevent becoming a full-blown TPFA dad is to remember the old adage: our children learn what they live. If we don't want our daughters to grow up expecting to do everything at home or our sons to grow up with the idea that participation in family life is optional, then we need to model presence.

The reality is that while Modern Dads are doing more, the research consistently shows that women (working or not) continue to do the vast majority of housework and child-related tasks.[4] Whatever the family structure and no matter who is the breadwinner, dads need to model full participation in home life. In some cases, this may mean both men and women have to step out of their comfort zones. For example, it is just as difficult for my wife to let go of doing the laundry as it is for me to initiate doing the laundry.

Now, a few words about limit setting.

My colleague Terry Real says, "Our relationship to our children is essentially like our other relationship to anyone else, with one striking difference: our children are clearly not our peers." He

more >

describes parenting as an example of 'healthy hierarchy.' Being in the hierarchical position (the one in charge), he says, is both easier and more difficult than other relationships.[5]

It's easier, Real explains, because we don't look to our children to meet our dependency needs. We don't, for example, look to our children to ease our worries about our finances or motivate us when we feel down. Consequently, they don't disappoint us in ways a spouse or friend can by not meeting our needs. With our children we can truly love unconditionally. However, being in charge is more difficult than our other relationships because it requires that we show up, take leadership and be 'on watch' at all times.

There is nothing wrong with being friendly (sharing interests, spending time together, etc.) but children need and want their father to be a parent, not a friend. Unfortunately, some dads today forget this important distinction. While this happens for many reasons - the dad has poor boundaries, lacks other adult male friendships, can't tolerate not being liked, leaves the limit-setting for his partner to do, etc. - I often find the underlying issues to be about guilt or fear. Guilt for not being around enough and/or fear of having the same distant relationship his own father may have had with him. So, naturally, being a friend or 'fun dad' is easier than being the bad guy.

Bad guys have to show up and set firm, consistent and fair limits on a child. To *not* do so is a form of neglect and sets children up to think they are above the rules. Being too authoritative, on the other hand, can actually create more problems than solutions.

There are volumes written on limit-setting, so in the following action I've boiled it down to some of the essentials.

Finally, showing up at school is key to your child's academic success and social-emotional development. It is important to look at *how* and *how often* you get involved at school. The following actions will help you evaluate your level of involvement as well as explore ways you can show up for your child at school.

ACTION #1
Set Limits: Be a Parent, Not a Friend

From a young age, children will test to see exactly how well their parents set limits. The eternal question most of us ask is "Am I being too easy or too strict?" Unfortunately, there is no easy answer to this question. However, in the following section, you will be presented with 5 key dimensions of limit-setting.

Please do the following:

STEP 1:   Read the following 5 key dimensions to limit setting and give yourself a letter grade for each (A - F, or whatever grading system you're familiar with).

STEP 2:   Discuss the grades you gave yourself with your child's mother (or your partner) or a trusted friend who knows you as a parent. Ask them if they agree/disagree about the grades you gave yourself.

1   **I am willing to make my child uncomfortable.**

Tolerating a young child's tears when we say 'no' or an older child's anger when we revoke a privilege is difficult. A child's reaction can cause the sternest disciplinarian to second-guess himself. Setting limits, however, requires that we not fear our children's response, no matter how angry or upset they appear to be. Children who go unchallenged become adults who think they are above the rules. This is a set-up because, as we know, the adult world has plenty of rules. It is our duty to let them know actions have consequences in the short and long-term.

Your willingness to tolerate your children's discomfort is greatly affected by your experience growing up. If you are from a dysfunctional family (eg. a father who let you get away with anything or a mother who was strict to the point of being cruel) your tendency as a parent will likely be to repeat that behavior, do the opposite or vacillate between the two.[6]

For example, Glenn had a father who used anger and intimidation to set limits. As a dad today, he tends to over-indulge his children. This is often an unconscious reaction to his upbringing; he doesn't want his kids to experience him as cruel, as he did his own father. At times, he also swings in the other direction and can be overly stern, repeating the exact behavior he disliked in his father.

The more dysfunctional the upbringing, the more critical it is to understand your potential patterns. If you want to make sure you're doing your best, I recommend getting support from a partner, other dads, parenting books, community resources, and/or a professional.

Grade: ___

2   I give my children choices instead of orders.

It's our job to draw (and re-draw) the line for what is acceptable and unacceptable behavior from our children. We must also communicate the consequences for stepping over that line. We then leave the choice - whether or not to step over that line - up to our children.

Another common approach is to use control - simply telling a child what to do or not do. If they don't comply, they face consequences. While some situations require us to use control (i.e., safety concerns, timing, etc.), as an overall approach to discipline it's ineffective, inefficient and often backfires. In the long run, controlling a child teaches blind obedience and often leads to more rebellious behavior. Control also fails to promote independent thinking and personal responsibility.

TEENAGE EXAMPLE:

Control: "Turn off the television and come to dinner right now! How many times do I have to say it!"

Choice: "Dinner is ready now. You have to the count of five to shut off the TV, wash up and sit at the table. If you don't, there will be no more TV for the rest of the night. You decide."

CHILD EXAMPLE:

Control: "Sarah, you have to share with your friend. Give her a turn."

Choice: "Sarah, if you would rather play alone, we'll ask your friend to go home. If you want your friend to stay, you need to share your toys. What would you like to do?"

In the moment, we usually don't want to have a lengthy conversation about why coming to dinner or sharing is important. So keep it brief. But a larger discussion with our children - at the right time and place - about why we set certain limits is critical. Children need to understand, for example, why sharing is a vital part of friendship or promptness to a family meal is important. Another name for this discussion is called *transmitting our values.* Children deserve to understand why we do what we do. Now, if that same discussion, whether about sharing or coming to dinner on time, has to happen more than a few times, the message may not be getting through. And if the message isn't getting through, chances are the consequences are not serious enough.

Grade: ___

3   **I do my best to ensure the consequence fits the crime.**

A teenager who stays out too late one night, can't go out the next. The young child who won't clean up her toys gets one taken away. The young teen who doesn't call to check in, loses phone privileges. In the moment it's not always easy to be so logical, especially when a child's behavior is flagrant. Which is why it's perfectly legitimate to take a little time, think it through, or consult with a partner/trusted friend before you give the consequence.

Making the consequence fit the crime is as much for our benefit as theirs. The more unreasonable the consequence, the less likely our children are to comply and the harder the follow-through is for us. "If you are late again, you aren't going out for the rest of the year!" is likely to be impossible to enforce. Generally, the younger the child, the more concrete and immediate the consequences must be.

An important lesson I learned working in a group home for troubled teens was that the consequence has to be something the child cares about and causes some degree of discomfort or inconvenience. If taking your four-year-old son's toy away doesn't bother him, or staying in on a Saturday night is not a discomfort to your teen daughter, you've missed the mark. This is a clear sign you need to turn up the heat.

If, however, you escalate the consequences and your child continues to make poor choices, it is essential to seek outside help or support.

Grade: ___

4   **I follow through with consequences and rewards.**

There is no more efficient and effective way to guarantee a lifetime of headaches than to not follow through with a consequence. Being 'all bark but no bite' sends a clear message to children that at the end of the day they can pretty much do as they darn well please. Following through with a consequence can be difficult for three main reasons: we have to tolerate our children's reactions (anger, disappointment, etc.), we have to trust in our own judgment, and we actually have to do what we said we were going to do. Again, this is much easier to do if we give our children consequences that are reasonable and 'fit the crime.'

With all this talk of consequence, crime and punishment, I don't want to leave out the power of rewards. I am not opposed to motivating children by using incentives. Of course, this can be a slippery slope. Do you want your son to earn good grades even if he's doing it for the pair of sneakers you've promised him? Philosophically this is a tough call. I've known rewards to work very well with children who have gotten into difficulty and needed some strong motivation to pull themselves out. Yet, overdoing the rewards can teach children that what matters is the destination and not the journey, the end and not the means.

Grade: ___

ACTION #2
Evaluate the Division of Housework and Child Care in Your Family

The following action is intended to raise your awareness about the division of labor in your family. If you are in a two-parent family, pay attention to the balance of responsibilities between you and your partner. Even if your partner stays at home, it is important to model some degree of equality. Children need to learn that men's work at home is not limited to stereotypical tasks such as taking out the garbage and paying the bills. If you are a single dad who does everything on these lists, take a moment to think about where you may find more support.

Take an inventory of child and home-related tasks by circling a dot on the scale.

Child-related Tasks:	mostly dad		about even		mostly mom
Purchases your children's clothes?	●	●	●	●	●
Schedules doctor appointments?	●	●	●	●	●
Makes childcare arrangements?	●	●	●	●	●
Bathes and gets younger kids ready for bed?	●	●	●	●	●
Arranges social plans (play dates, etc.)?	●	●	●	●	●
Monitors curfews of older children?	●	●	●	●	●
Who checks-in with your older children?	●	●	●	●	●
Sets limits with the children?	●	●	●	●	●
Maintains contact with your child's school?	●	●	●	●	●

House-related Tasks:	mostly dad		about even		mostly mom
Does the laundry and cleans house?	●	●	●	●	●
Takes out the garbage?	●	●	●	●	●
Cleans the bathrooms?	●	●	●	●	●
Makes lunches?	●	●	●	●	●
Makes the beds?	●	●	●	●	●
Vacuums and Dusts?	●	●	●	●	●
Does outside maintenance?	●	●	●	●	●
Makes sure children do their chores?	●	●	●	●	●
Does the food shopping?	●	●	●	●	●
Cooks family meals?	●	●	●	●	●
Cleans up after family meals?	●	●	●	●	●
Does the finances?	●	●	●	●	●
Buys gifts and writes thank you notes?	●	●	●	●	●

Reflection III

Showing Up at School

Dads today are far more involved in schools than ever before, though not necessarily in ways that benefit children most. Showing up for sporting events, the occasional parent-teacher conference, or a discipline meeting is not enough. Research shows when dads volunteer at the school, attend class or whole school events, show up for conferences and get involved in the PTA/PA/Dad's Club, children are more likely to:[7]

- *Get better grades.*
- *Go further with their education.*
- *Enjoy school more.*
- *Develop healthy peer relationships.*

The benefits to us as dads include:

- *Better understanding of our children's culture & day-to-day life (friends, teachers, activities, etc.).*
- *Chance to develop relationships with adults in child's life (teachers, other parents, etc.).*
- *Model community involvement.*

I could go on about the benefits to you, your children, the school community, mothers and even other children at school, but none of this matters much if we don't address the barriers:

- *Time: "I would love to, I'm just too busy."*
- *Environment: "I don't want to be the only guy."*
- *Your child's mother: "That's my domain."*
- *Your child: "It's embarrassing."*

While there are real barriers, the bottom line is we must creatively find solutions to get more involved at school. Talk to your child's school about having a parent education night for dads. Attend a PTA/PA meeting with another dad. Talk with your child's mother (or your partner) about the benefits of involvement. Organize a community service event at the school for dads and children. Just as schools could reach out more to dads, we could also raise the bar and expect more from ourselves.

A note about the difference between school involvement when children are in lower/middle versus high school.
Parent involvement drops off radically when children enter high school. However, it is a huge mistake to think your involvement in the high school years is any less important; if anything, it's more important. If your child's high school does not foster parent involvement, speak up. There are limits to our involvement, but most educators understand the home connection is critical. Your child may not want you involved, but there are ways to act more behind the scenes.

The Modern Dads Club

More and more schools today have dad's groups. While their purpose can vary widely, most groups plan activities, do community service and meet periodically. Having worked with many groups across the country, I've created a guideline for starting a Modern Dads Club. It can also be used to enhance an existing group. Email john@johnbadalament.com for info.

ACTION #1
Assess Your Level of Involvement in Your Child's School

The following table will help you look specifically at your current level of school involvement. Comparing your involvement in your child's school vs. your father's involvement in your school will quickly highlight the similarities and differences.

Simply write in the appropriate number in each of the boxes. When finished, compare the results and decide if you should change your level of participation.

For some context, here's how to view the range you fall within:

7 to 11
You need to do more, get going.

12 to 17
You're on the right track, keep going.

18 to 21
You're actively involved, good going.

Enter the appropriate number in the boxes below

1 = **RARELY**   2 = **SOMETIMES**   3 = **FREQUENTLY**

	YOUR DAD	YOU
Drop-off/ Pick-up child		
Parent-Teacher Conferences		
Volunteer at School		
Parent Association Meetings		
Parent Education Events (i.e., speakers)		
Class-level Events (i.e., science night)		
Whole-school Events (sports, drama, clubs)		
TOTAL		

ACTION #2
Explore Different Ways to Get Involved at School

This action will help you discover the range of ways you could be involved and, more importantly, what your child's school needs from you and other dads. Chances are you could be more involved in your child's school experience. Or, maybe it's *how* you're involved that needs to change. Instead of attending conferences and sporting events, maybe you want to attend a parent night or volunteer your skills. If you are absolutely doing a great job already, this action will serve to increase your knowledge about your child's school.

Now it's time to go on a fact-finding mission. In order to learn about the many ways dads can get involved at school, do all four of the actions in the chart on the following page.

TEACHERS

Talk with at least 3 other dads about what they do (or know about). These might be dads you already know or you may step out and meet some new ones.

OTHER DADS

Meet or talk with your child's teacher or a school administrator about ways they've seen dads get more involved and what needs they have.

PTA MEETING

Attend a PTO/PA meeting at least once. Find out about activities and events in which you could participate. Pay attention to the number of dads present.

MOTHER

Talk with your child's mother (if not possible, a mother you know) about dad involvement from the mom's perspective - Is it important? Would it be welcomed?

IDEAS: _____

_____

_____

_____

_____

ACTION #3
Commit to Get Involved at School

Write down at least 2 concrete ways you intend to get involved in your child's school over the next six months. If you are already very involved, consider trying something different.

I suggest making these commitments along with another dad from your child's school. Another dad will help with motivation, especially if father involvement at the school is low.

1

2

The Second Practice: Showing Up Physically

End of Practice Commitments

Based on what you've learned in The Second Practice, consider making 2 to 3 commitments to yourself, your children or any other important people in your life. Write in as little or as much detail as necessary:

1

2

3

The Third Practice
Connecting Emotionally

When I first present the idea of "Connecting Emotionally" to an auditorium of mostly dads, one question, whether spoken or not, always seems to hang in the air: is this going to get 'touchy-feely?' However, when it comes to discussing the kind of relationship we envision with our children, most dads will say without hesitation they want to feel close and connected. This captures one of the central dilemmas for so many Modern Dads: the so-called 'feminine' or 'touchy-feely' qualities we were raised to devalue, mock or avoid – emotionality, vulnerability, sensitivity – are the very qualities we both want and need as dads. In this practice, you will learn that connecting emotionally requires not only courage and skill, but a willingness to let down your guard.

The research is clear: a close, emotionally connected father-child relationship is a form of prevention and source of health and happiness for both child and father. Renowned researcher John Gottman found that children with emotionally available dads do better in school, have better peer relationships, and relate better with teachers than children with more emotionally distant dads. Children with dads who are critical or dismissing of emotions are more likely to do poorly in school, fight more with friends and have poor health.[8] The National Longitudinal Study of Adolescent Health found the single most protective factor for reducing behavioral risks, such as drug and alcohol use, early sexual activity, smoking and depression, is a child's connectedness to their parents; fathers were noted as being of particular importance.

The research is clear: A close, emotionally connected father-child relationship is a form of prevention as well as a predictable source of health and happiness.

Interestingly, a U.S. National Institute of Mental Health study found that fathers who were actively involved in their children's lives had fewer accidental deaths, fewer premature deaths, less substance abuse and fewer hospital admissions.[9] Not only is a close father-child relationship good for children, but it's a positive aspect of men's physical and mental health as well.

more >

The emotional connection between a father and his child can begin at birth. So, what exactly does it mean to connect emotionally and most importantly, *how* does one connect? In this practice, you will be introduced to a simple, easy-to-remember model for connecting emotionally: *know, be known, and keep the lines of communication open.* By knowing our children - becoming experts about their lives - we send them a clear message that they are important. Beyond our focus and attention, knowing requires being a skilled listener. In this practice you will learn about the Four Classic Listeners.

The second part of connecting emotionally is being known. This involves us sharing more about who we are as men - not just as 'dad' - with our children. By using the power of storytelling, you will connect to many important themes in your child's life, such as dealing with peer pressure, facing and overcoming challenges, crushes and dating, etc. Letting your children know more about what you think and feel on a regular basis is essential to building a healthy connection.

Finally, you will learn how to keep the lines of communication open with children of all ages... no matter what. This two-pronged approach addresses the importance of Daily Dialogue as well as Regular Heart-to-Heart talks. Using a powerful communication tool called the Modern Dads Relationship Inventory™ will not only help you and your child stay connected, but will allow you to model essential relationship skills in the process.

Reflection I

Knowing
Your Children

Think about the people in the world you feel closest to. What accounts for that connection? Why do you feel so close? Likely, you'd say that this person really gets you - knows what makes you tick, knows your flaws and loves you anyway.

Children crave and developmentally need this same feeling from their dads. They need us to know who they are as unique individuals and be experts about their lives - what scares them or brings them joy, what a certain look on their face means, what they're doing in school, how they cope with stress, who their friends are, etc. By being experts, we send a clear, powerful message that they are worthy of our time, interest, and attention to detail. In short, it builds their sense of self-worth at any age.

If our sons and daughters don't feel like we know them, chances are they won't tell us, they will act it out. A young child may seek a dad's attention by becoming more defiant. A middle schooler may develop an eating disorder or lose interest in academics. A teenager may experiment with drugs and alcohol. Or, a child at any age may quietly give up trying, thinking instead she is not worthy of her dad's attention and interest.

As dads, we are mirrors for our children, especially when they are young. For example, if they look in our mirror and see a dad who appreciates their quirky sense of humor, they may think 'I must be funny and a good person to hang out with.' By contrast, if they look at the mirror and see a dad who makes empty promises and is always busy, they may think 'maybe I'm not that interesting?' or 'maybe I'm really not good enough for him?'

What about children who don't want us to know them? Naturally, as children enter adolescence they want more independence. Even when they resist, push away, or shut us out, it does not mean we don't matter anymore. A father will always matter to his children. Giving them more space and privacy does not mean we have to stop being interested or aware of what is happening in their lives.

Studies done with teens show they really do want parents involved in their lives. In her study of fathers and sons, researcher Ricky Pelach-Galil found that around age 13-14 the father became a central figure in boys' lives.[10] The boys reported paying close attention to their father's habits, values, and routines, as well as *his* interest in *their* lives. This is, of course, the same age when boys are pushing away from their parents to be with their friends.

Daughters are no different. In a survey of 8th-12th grade girls done by the National Center for Fathering, daughters consistently said they wanted more time with their fathers, better communication, and a sense that their fathers were interested in their lives.[11] As one girl said, "I wish my father would try to understand me more."

To truly know our children the most important skill we need is listening. The following actions will test your knowledge of your children and show you an approach to being a skilled listener. The Fourth Practice (Modeling Healthy Relationships) will present additional listening skills to those below.

ACTION #1
Take The Quiz:
How Well do You Know Your Children?

Most of us think we know our kids pretty well, sometimes even better than they know themselves, right? Well, in order to test our knowledge, I have developed a short quiz for dads to take. For some, this will be simple; if so, consider it an affirmation of what a great parent you are. For others, especially dads with limited contact with their children, this will be a more difficult exercise; use the quiz as a reminder, motivator or wake-up call.

Take the following quiz alone. Answer all the questions you can for each of your children. When you finish, check your answers by talking directly with your child, your child's mother or your partner. Make sure you fill in any questions you got wrong or left blank.

1) What recent accomplishment is your child most proud of?

2) Name one of your child's big disappointments this year?

3) What are your child's current prized possessions?

4) What is your child's favorite food?

5) Can you name your child's teachers?

6) Name 2 things your child did at school in the past 2 weeks:

7) What is most challenging about school for your child?

8) What does your child like about school?

9) What does your child like to do in their spare time?

10) What types of music does your child listen to?

11) Which TV shows, movies, actors/characters and athletes are popular with your child and his/her friends?

12) What are his/her 3 favorite websites to visit?

13) Does your child belong to any social networking websites (MySpace, Facebook, etc.)?

14) What causes your child the greatest stress?

15) Who are your child's close friends & why does he/she like them?

16) Who are your child's heroes and role models?

17) What would your child like to be when he/she grows up?

18) What is something that really upsets your child?

19) What does your child like to do with you?

20) What does your child love about you?

ACTION #2
Practice the Essentials of Listening

How well we choose to listen or not is often a matter of situation and context. For example, when pulled over for speeding, I can suddenly become the most attentive listener you've ever seen. An hour later that attentiveness may disappear. For example, I may find myself listening to my daughter's story with one ear and listening to the baseball game on TV with the other. It's important to remember, we all have the capacity to be great listeners. Listening is a powerful form of caretaking and can greatly affect your child's sense of self-worth at any age. It's another way of saying 'you are important.' To be most effective, however, requires figuring out what kind of listening is needed. The following steps outline essential skills as well as *how* and *when* to use them with children and adults.

STEP 1

Read the following rules for listening situations. These are some general guidelines for being a skilled listener.

1. **Listen for main ideas and feelings.**
    Pay attention to the important points your child is trying to make. What does he want you to 'get?' Also, be aware of and acknowledge the emotions your child expresses. Similarly, if you think she is withholding expression, simply mention it. For younger children this is especially critical; they need their parents to label and validate their feelings.

2. **As the listener, don't become the speaker.**
   As a listener, it's always tempting to want to relate your own story, give your opinion, or offer a solution. As a general rule, allow for breathing space or even silence before responding. There is nothing more frustrating than when the listener becomes the speaker. It is especially important to resist using what your child says as a springboard for teaching a lesson.

3. **If unsure what the speaker needs from you, ask!**
   Sometimes a speaker wants to be listened to in a specific way; she may want you to give some advice, share your experience or just be a sounding board and say nothing. If you're uncertain what's needed, a way to prevent the speaker from getting frustrated with you is to simply ask:

   "How can I be most helpful? Should I offer solutions, not say anything and just nod, share my own similar experiences?"

4. **Don't agree to be a listener if the time is not right.**
   Let's say you come home from work and your child (or partner) wants to talk or just starts talking. You start listening, but really you just want to relax a few minutes first. Instead of just 'yes-ing' them, be direct and say when you'll be more available to listen. Setting this kind of boundary is helpful to children of all ages.

   "I want to hear all about it! If you can give me five minutes to kick off my shoes, I'll be all ears. Sound good?"

STEP 2

Review the following descriptions of the Four Classic Types of Listeners and determine which one(s) you most relate to. Then, assign each of the four a percentage to indicate how often you become that type of listener with your child. *Optional: ask your partner to assign percentages for you.*

THE JOURNALIST

If there is one kind of listener that's a good default, it's The Journalist. The Journalist asks good questions, some open-ended ('how are things with your friends?') others closed ('did you have a good time?'). His body language lets the speaker know he is tuned-in. He makes eye contact, nods, and his facial expressions ebb and flow with the speaker's words. He clarifies what the speaker says with an occasional 'is that right?' He also listens for what's *not* being said. The result is the speaker feels very attended to, taken care of, and focused on. Young children, especially, need The Journalist.

I am this type of listener ____% of the time

THE STORYTELLER

He relates to what the other person is saying by sharing his own similar (or sometimes not) stories. Sharing experiences is a great way to show empathy, that you really 'get it.' If you start telling stories as the listener, however, it's easy for the speaker to feel like you're interested in yourself, not them.

I am this type of listener ____% of the time

THE VACATIONER

He is not really present for the speaker. Though he may appear to be listening, he is actually vacationing in his mind - thinking about work, somewhere he'd rather be or what the score of the game is. This kind of listening can be great if the speaker simply wants to spew words or talk at someone, anyone. However, most people don't like talking with someone who is not really there. Usually, a speaker can tell when they are talking to The Vacationer.

I am this type of listener ____% of the time

THE HANDYMAN

This is the kind of listening, stereotypically speaking, guys tend to like. The Handyman is useful. He's ready to fix any problem. He nods and listens intently, mainly with an ear towards what he can offer. The advantage of The Handyman is sometimes people want to hear solutions and really feel like they are being heard. On the downside, sometimes people just want to be heard, not fixed.

I am this type of listener ____% of the time

STEP 3
Review the four essential skills for listening below.

Ⓒ CONFIRM what you hear by reflecting back to the speaker.
When relevant, repeat what you heard the speaker say (use your words to describe what you hear). The key is to ask the speaker if you got it right, if you are on track. This is especially important to do with young children.

"I hear you saying _____ , have I got that right?"
"So, you did _____ and then you said _____ , does that capture it?"

Ⓐ ASK questions for clarification.
When you ask questions it shows that you're interested and following what the speaker is saying. Also, clarifying what happened or what a person is feeling gives you important information about the situation.

"What did you do after that?"
"What were you feeling at that point?"

Ⓡ RELATE personally to what they are saying.
Let the speaker know you understand what they are going through. This helps the speaker both know you're listening, but also not feel so alone. Even if you don't share exactly the same experience, you can generalize (example #2 below). Be careful, though, not to turn the attention to yourself and stay focused on the speaker.

"I hear you. I've been let down before too."
"You're not the only one who's ever had that happen."

Ⓞ OFFER your perspective, thoughts, impressions, suggestions.
Sometimes children won't ask, but want to hear what you have to say. It's best to not to assume you know what they want. Instead, make an offer:

"Is there anything you need or anything I can do?"
"Would you like to hear what I think about what you said?"

STEP 4

Based on which of the Four Classic Types of Listeners you most identify with, read below to learn how you can incorporate the essential skills.

IF YOU ARE THE JOURNALIST Ⓒ Ⓐ Ⓡ Ⓞ

The Journalist incorporates all four of the essential skills. If you identify most with The Journalist, you're on the right track. Don't forget to pay attention to what kind of listening the speaker seems to want most.

⬇ ⬇ ↓ ↓

IF YOU ARE THE HANDYMAN Ⓒ Ⓐ Ⓡ Ⓞ

The best strategy for The Handyman is to work on **confirming** what you're hearing and **asking** questions of the speaker. These two skills will keep you focused on the speaker and away from your own story and your advice. When he is sure the speaker feels heard, The Handyman can then **offer** to share his perspective.

⬇ ⬇ ↓ ↓

IF YOU ARE THE STORYTELLER Ⓒ Ⓐ Ⓡ Ⓞ

Like The Handyman, The Storyteller needs to work on bringing the focus back to the speaker. The best strategies for The Storyteller are to focus on **confirming** and **asking**. When he is certain the speaker feels heard, The Storyteller can **relate** or even **offer** to relate a personal story or example.

⬇ ↓ ⬇ ↓

IF YOU ARE THE VACATIONER Ⓒ Ⓐ Ⓡ Ⓞ

The Vacationer could really use any of the four skills to bring him back to the present moment. However, the practice of **confirming** what is being said requires the most attention. Another strategy for The Vacationer is to work on **relating** personal stories to what the speaker is saying. By relating your own story, you push yourself into being engaged in what is being said.

Reflection II

Being Known
by Your Children

When I go to schools I often ask students to anonymously write down two questions they have for their dad, but never asked. I collect the questions. Periodically, I have tallied the responses in order to find the most popular questions. Surprisingly, the most common questions had nothing to do with sex or drug use. The two most popular questions consistently were: What was his relationship like with his dad? And, what was he like as a kid? These and all the questions children have for their fathers point to what I call the elephant in the living room of child development: the missing stories of men's lives, particularly men's emotional lives. Children not only want, but need their father's stories to understand who they are and where they come from.

Storytelling is a great way for dads to connect emotionally with their kids. Children want real stories about who you were (and are) as a person, not just as their dad. War stories can be fun, but I'm talking about letting them into your experiences with winning and losing, being embarrassed and having anxiety, overcoming challenges and giving up. But which stories are appropriate and which are inappropriate to share with a child? The short answer is, trust your gut. If your gut says telling a story about your father's drinking will be upsetting, don't tell it. If, however, you have a history of your gut getting you into trouble, then first check it out with a trusted friend or partner. While there are no hard and fast rules for storytelling, here are a few guidelines:

Let your stories emerge naturally, in context; don't overwhelm your child with your entire life story on a Saturday afternoon.

> Your daughter loses a game: "Did I ever tell you about what my dad used to do when I would lose?"

Don't always be a reactive storyteller; take the lead.

> "When I was in fifth grade, I was really concerned with what other people thought of me... do you ever feel that way?"

Share stories about your present, not just your past.

> "Sometimes I have trouble keeping my mouth shut. I was in this meeting the other day..."

Include feelings in your stories, not just facts.

> Children need to know that you get scared, worried, joyful, etc. By labeling your feelings, you help children understand their own.

Be mindful of how your stories may be used against you.

> If you decide to tell your teenage son about past alcohol or drug use, I suggest you prepare a response for when/if your son uses that story to justify his own use.

When telling stories about your own father, keep in mind your child's relationship to their grandfather.

> If your child has a more positive relationship with your dad than you did, do not to divide your child's loyalties. Talk more about the things you are trying to do differently. If your father was abusive, seek professional advice before sharing such stories.

Remember that stories are the lifeblood connecting generations. Stories are gifts every child deserves. The following actions will help you connect with your own stories and determine which to share with your children.

ACTION #1
Give the Gift of Your Story

On the following page is a grid meant to prompt you into thinking of stories you can share with your child about your life. Each story topic (left column) also has a writing prompt next to it.* You may choose to write down some of your stories and keep them as a journal for your children. Or, you could write these stories as letters to your child in an effort to help them learn more about you. This is an especially good idea for those of you with young children. Finally, find appropriate moments or use ritual time (see The Second Practice) to share the stories of your life.

Try to tell stories about yourself when you were your child's current age.

---

* *Some of the prompts are from my friend and colleague Nancy Aronie, author of "Writing From The Heart." For anyone interested in her fantastic creative writing workshops please visit Nancy's website: www.chilmarkwritingworkshop.com*

STORY TOPIC	WRITING PROMPT
Family Relationships	Dinner at my home growing up...
Friendships	When I was young, my friends...
School	If my teachers only knew...
Work	The best/worst job I ever had...
Self-esteem	I felt good/bad about myself...
Body Image/Puberty	When I looked in the mirror...
Making Decisions	I knew it had to be done, but...
Peer Pressure/Fitting in	I knew if I didn't...
Competition	My thrill of victory/agony of defeat...
Interests	Nothing excited me more than...
Attraction/Dating	My first crush...
Sex	Something I wish I knew then...
Spirituality	I believe...
Being Irresponsible	I can't believe I...
Money	I've learned that money...
Popular Culture	I would do anything to listen/see...

ACTION #2
Practice Identifying and Naming What You Feel

In this action you will practice paying attention to your feelings and thoughts on a daily basis for the next 21 days (the time it takes to develop a new habit). Being able to identify, name and express one's feelings is a skill that many of us, as boys, didn't fully learn because feelings were often thought of as 'unmanly'. Consequently, as men, some may find it challenging to practice emotional awareness or even understand why it's important. If we want to be known by others, it's important to know ourselves. By honing this skill we can become less reactive when faced with conflict, more attentive to our own (and other's) needs, and ultimately healthier in all of our relationships. As dads, it is also our responsibility to prepare our children by modeling the skills they will need as adults.

Please do the three steps on the following pages.

This action is adapted from Terry Real's book *The New Rules of Marriage: A Breakthrough Program for 21st Century Relationships*

1. **Review the Seven Primary Emotions**[12] Like primary colors, these seven emotions are the source for all other emotions. For example, anxiety comes from fear and pride comes from joy.

2. Check your feelings three times during your day.

Do this for the next 21 days. In your mind simply freeze whatever you're thinking or doing for a moment and ask yourself "What am I feeling right now, this second?" Choose from the list of Primary Emotions.

For example, you might say to yourself:

"Right now, I just dropped my son off at school and I feel..."

JOY
about the talk we had
in the car ride to school.

PAIN
(disappointment) about the
difficulty he's having at school.

ANGER
at the guy in front of me
driving too slowly.

3. **Remember the following tips:**

- **Your emotions don't have to be big.**
  You can feel a little of this and a little of that.

- **Your emotions don't have to be consistent.**
  We handle this by saying, "A part of me," as in, "A part of me feels excited about being with the guys and hanging out someplace nice. And another part of me already misses the kids."

- **Don't judge yourself for feeling one way or another; just be aware.**

- **Typically, how we *think* about something will determine how we *feel* about it.**

- **When you feel something but don't know why, pause to trace the thoughts and actions that led up to this moment.**
  For example, let's say you identify that you're feeling disappointed but don't know why. You might then say to yourself, "A minute ago I was at work. Before that I was on the phone with my wife. We were talking about having to cancel our vacation... That's it! I'm disappointed about the trip!" Once you know the thought that triggered the feeling, you can try and reframe it or think differently: "Actually, since we're not going away I can get stuff done at home."

Reflection III

Keeping the Lines of Communication Open

The idea of knowing and being known gives you a sense of the big picture (the macro) for connecting emotionally with your children. In this last part of the practice you will be introduced to specific, unique communication skills (the micro) to keep your connection strong: Daily Dialogue and Regular Heart-to-Hearts.

Daily Dialogue is a particular kind of check-in to do with your child. With young children, this will help you establish an effective way to keep the lines of communication open early on. With teens, this skill is a potential antidote to the one-word answers (fine/good/nothing) parents get when they ask questions about their child's life. If Daily Dialogue is the short-term approach to keeping lines of communication open, then having a Regular Heart-to-Heart is the long-term approach.

A Regular Heart-to-Heart is a way for you and your child to talk consistently and honestly about the quality of your relationship. It also provides you both with a built-in mechanism for handling difficult conversations. Many men think of a heart-to-heart as that dramatic, confrontational moment when a man and his father finally open up to each other. This is about normalizing the conversation. No drama. No conflict. No years of silence.

In order to make the Regular Heart-to-Heart easier and more structured, I've developed The Relationship Inventory. Father and child individually take stock of their relationship by answering questions, then sharing their answers. By using this simple, yet powerful tool regularly (3 times each year), dads will:

Teach children to have high standards for relationships

How we treat our children from an early age becomes a standard for how they expect to be treated in all their relationships, from friendship to dating to marriage. By encouraging your daughter to address problems directly with you - despite her fear - she learns not to silence herself in any relationship. By listening to your son's feelings, he learns to expect others to be present for him as well. By respecting their individuality and point of view, we teach children to insist on being treated well by others.

Build trust by staying accountable for the job you do as a dad

We don't often think of adults needing to be accountable to children. But if we want our children to trust and respect us, staying accountable - taking responsibility for the effect of our words and actions - is essential. A dad who rages at his children can stay accountable by getting help. A dad who rarely sees his children (due to work, separation, etc.) can stay accountable by letting his children know he understands their pain or anger. The tricky thing about staying accountable to a child is that we don't always know how our behavior impacts them; they won't necessarily say, 'your anger really frightens me.' In fact, they're more likely to remain silent and take it out on themselves or others. The Relationship Inventory provides a structured way for children to tell us how well we're handling our job as dads.

Give them the foundations of relationship literacy

When you were young, how did you learn about relationships? Maybe you watched the adults in your home or friends' homes, learned from TV, movies and health class, or took in some teachings through your religion. Chances are you didn't receive much formal instruction. Even today, most children are still not taught relationship skills in any comprehensive way. The Relationship Inventory emphasizes certain foundations of relationship literacy: self-reflection, giving and receiving feedback, getting your needs met, and listening, to name a few.

Teach children the disappearing art of reflection

In this age of email, IM, and MySpace it's easy for children to react without thinking, reveal too much about themselves too quickly, and develop a false sense of connection with someone they may not know very well. The Relationship Inventory helps teach them to slow down and reflect on themselves and their relationships.

ACTION #1
Initiate Daily Dialogue:
The Successful 5 Minute Check-In

Initiating a daily 5 minute check-in is an important aspect of staying connected emotionally with a child at any age (including infants). The content of what's said during this time is less important than your presence and attention. Even if you don't see your child every day, this can be done on the phone or Internet. The daily check-in is most effective when done as a ritual before or after dinner, just before bedtime (good for younger kids), or even in the morning. While competing schedules often make this difficult, do your best to be consistent. During your daily check-in your attention should be fully on your child.

Review the following elements of a successful check-in. While these suggestions are for a verbal check-in, just spending quiet, focused time together is equally as important.

For infants and toddlers or less verbal children, your check-in can take the form of uninterrupted play, a shared activity or face-to-face time (get down on their level, make eye contact and focus on your child).

STEP 1 | Review the rules for a successful check-in

1. **Say something nice about your child** | Children of all ages need to hear praise from their father. Appreciate something they've done, recognize a quality they possess, or remind them how much you love them. At the very least, pay them a simple compliment.

2. **Ask relevant, not generic questions** | Remember earlier in the practice I said you should be an expert about your child's life? Well, your questions should demonstrate your expertise. Instead of 'how was school?' ask about her science project or the teacher he can't stand. Also, instead of direct questions, try asking open-ended questions about their friends or a particular friend. This can feel less intrusive and get them talking.

3. **Don't Just *Do* Something, *Sit There*** | There is no quicker way to shut down a conversation with a young person than when you try to fix their problems or turn what they say into a lecture or a 'teachable moment.' If you must, ask if they would like to hear your advice. For further explanation, go back to Reflection I and do all the actions.

4. **Relate something about your day** | As a middle-school girl once said in my father-daughter workshop, "Maybe if he would talk about *his* day, I wouldn't give short answers like 'fine' or 'nothing'." I use the word *relate* because when talking about your day with a child you must find common ground. She is more likely to be interested if you share personal experiences instead of events or 'what happened at work.' Consider talking about these areas of your day:

CHALLENGES | "I've been trying to exercise four days a week, but today I didn't want to go. Do you ever break promises to yourself?"

FEELINGS | "I felt so anxious about this project I had to complete." Or "When I finished the job, I felt so accomplished. When's the last time you felt good about something you finished?"

THOUGHTS | "At lunch, you know what I was thinking about? What a great basketball player you are."

STEP 2 | Discuss the check-in with your child

If you already do some form of a check-in, you may simply add some of the above elements without much discussion. If this is new or a big departure from your regular check-in, explain to your child that you would like to stay more informed about each other's lives on a daily basis. Also say that during the check-in time you will commit to giving your full attention – no interruptions, cell phones, TV, other conversations, etc. Assure your child that it won't simply be you grilling them with questions, rather that you will say something about your day as well.

Ask your child what would make the check-in useful or fun for them. Find out what will make the check-in fail. Finally, be flexible and present it as an experiment. I suggest making a verbal agreement with your child to try the daily check-in for two weeks, even if the check-in has to be done by phone or email. With an agreement, you won't feel like you're pulling teeth.

If you face resistance, consider the following steps: first, think about what you may be doing to create the resistance (e.g., not showing up enough lately, losing your temper easily, being overly controlling). Next, listen to your child's reasons, discuss why it's important to you and find a compromise (maybe you check-in every 2-3 days). Finally, if all else fails, require it for two weeks (see Setting Limits in The Second Practice) and then reevaluate.

STEP 3 | Do the daily check-in for 2 weeks

The following is a list of format suggestions. You may use your own or brainstorm something with your child. Just make sure your time together is uninterrupted, even if you don't say much. Don't limit the check-in by only discussing events. Talk about thoughts and feelings too. Finally, change it up a bit, try something for one week and change it the next. Possible formats include:

- **What's Hot/What's Not**: Each of you shares a few hot (positive or exciting) things from the day and a few things that weren't so great.
- **High/Low**: Similar to what's hot/what's not, each of you share a few high points of your day and a few low points as well.
- **Appreciations**: Talk about a few things you each appreciated that day. You could appreciate a person, weather, actions, words, etc.
- **Action talk**: William Pollack, author of *Real Boys,* encourages fathers to *do something* while talking - shoot baskets, make something, take a walk, etc.[13] This works with girls as well. By focusing on *doing,* the child is more likely to talk freely.

AFTER TWO WEEKS

What's working:

What needs changing:

ACTION #2
Have a Regular Heart-to-Heart: The Modern Dads Relationship Inventory™

The Modern Dads Relationship Inventory is a series of questions designed to initiate and encourage ongoing dialogue between dads and children. It's a structured way to have a heart-to-heart talk about your lives and your relationship with each other.

STEP 1: PREPARE
To effectively introduce this activity to your child and make the most of the experience, you'll need a bit of preparation.

1. **Think about when and where you will do The Relationship Inventory and how you can make it special.**
    The Relationship Inventory should be done outside of the home. Consider taking a drive or a walk, sitting in a park, having a meal at a quiet restaurant, etc. Make sure there is enough privacy so your child will feel comfortable talking; a baseball game, crowded café or mall will likely be distracting and defeat the purpose. However, to make this a special event, you could go to a movie, a game or the mall after doing The Relationship Inventory.

2. **Introduce the idea to your child and expect resistance.**
    Tell your child about *The Modern Dads Handbook*. Describe The Relationship Inventory and your ideas for making it a special event; ask for their ideas. You may get some resistance, especially from a teenager. Explain that it's very easy, it would mean a lot to you, and they'll have a good time. When younger children resist, emphasize the fun part; with older children emphasize how important they are

to you, how time flies, and that you want to make the most of it. If necessary, use a food/fun bribe. As a last resort, require it, just as you would any other family obligation.

Note: if you get a great deal of resistance or think it would be better to ease into it, you can select a portion of the questions and shorten the activity. I recommend selecting some questions from each section. Also, I encourage you to eventually do the entire Relationship Inventory in one sitting.

STEP 2: DO THE RELATIONSHIP INVENTORY
Determine which version of The Relationship Inventory you will be using and carefully read through it.

pg 96	The Relationship Inventory for Children	Ages 5 - 10
pg 98	The Relationship Inventory for Teens	Ages 11 - 18

Each version has its own step-by-step instructions. Follow them closely so each of you gets enough time to speak.

The Relationship Inventory for Children

INSTRUCTIONS

Step 1   Photocopy this spread (pages 96 and 97) for you and your child. Use a pad of paper to write responses. Note the question # before each response.

Step 2   Together, read aloud all 19 questions to make sure you both understand what's being asked.

Step 3   DAD must assure his CHILD that it's safe to be honest. DAD MUST SAY: "I want you to answer honestly. I promise to listen without getting upset. What you think is important to me."

Step 4   Split up and write your answers to EVERY question alone. Agree to return in 20 minutes. If writing is problematic or your child needs help, simply talk through your responses.

QUESTIONS

SCHOOL, WORK & FRIENDS

1. A really important friend to me is _____ because...
2. I think my friends like me because...
3. Recently, my friends have been talking a lot about...
4. Something that my peers from school (for child) or work (for dad) do that I don't like or don't understand is...
5. Two things I like about school/work are...
6. If I could change one thing at school/work it would be...
7. CHILD: A current event happening in the world today that I am concerned or confused about is...
   DADS: A current event I've been wondering if you've been affected by is...

Step 5	When done, come back together. Agree on how much time you'll take to share your answers. I suggest at least 20 minutes. If possible, leave it open-ended.
Step 6	DAD shares his answer to Question #1.
Step 7	CHILD shares their answer to Question #1.
Step 8	Continue alternating responses to each question, in order, until finished.
Step 9	When listening, focus on what's being said, not what *you* want to say. Use good body language. Don't interrupt or ask too many questions.

YOU AND ME

8. Two qualities I like about myself are...
9. Two qualities I like about you are...
10. If I could change any two things about myself (attitude, appearance, behavior), I would change...
11. Something I'm very good at is...
12. Something I wish I was better at is...
13. Something I think you're very good at is...
14. FOR CHILD: Dad, when you were my age, were you...
    FOR DAD: When I was your age, I...
15. FOR CHILD: Something I've always wanted to know about our family (today or in the past) is...
    FOR DAD: Something I liked about my family life growing up and something that was challenging...
16. One of the nicest things you've done for me recently is...
17. One thing I could do to be a better child/dad is...
18. One thing you could do to be a better dad/child is...
19. I hope that we always...

The Relationship Inventory for Teens

INSTRUCTIONS

Step 1   Photocopy this spread (pages 98 and 99) for you and your child. Use a pad of paper to write responses. Note the question # before each response.

Step 2   Together, read aloud all 33 questions to make sure you both understand what's being asked.

Step 3   DAD must assure his TEEN that it's safe to be honest. DAD MUST SAY: "I really want you to answer these questions honestly. I promise to listen without getting defensive, angry or upset. You don't have to protect me from your honesty."

Step 4   Split up, find a quiet place and each write your answers to EVERY question alone. Agree to return in 30 to 45 minutes.

QUESTIONS

OUR LIVES

1. Two qualities I like about myself...
2. What I love and respect about you is...
3. If I could change one thing about myself (a quality, physical attribute, attitude, etc.), I would change...
4. Lately, something that's been going well at school (or work) is...
5. If I could do one day over again at school (or work) it would be...
6. I have recently felt worried or stressed-out about...
7. I think you have been worried or stressed-out about...
8. A friend that is very important to me these days is _____ because...
9. Recently, something my friends talk about a lot is...
10. Something happening in the world today (current events) that I think about a lot is...
11. A SMALL change in my life (a new routine, physical growth, new teacher/coach, a driver's license, etc.) that has affected me is...
12. A BIG change in my life (birth/death, family life, a move, work situation, friendship, health issue, etc.) that has affected me is...
13. FOR TEEN: Dad, when you were my age, how did you handle... FOR DAD: When I was your age, things that made my life great were... and things that made it challenging were...

Step 5	When done, come back together. Agree on how much time you'll take to share your answers. I suggest at least 30 minutes. If possible, leave it open-ended.
Step 6	DAD shares his answer to Question #1.
Step 7	TEEN shares their answer to Question #1.
Step 8	Continue alternating responses to each question, in order, until finished.
Step 9	Remember, focus on what's being said, not what you want to say. Use good body language. Don't interrupt or ask too many questions. Avoid getting defensive.

OUR RELATIONSHIP

14. Positive qualities I bring to our relationship are...
15. Positive qualities you bring to our relationship are...
16. Something I really enjoy doing with you is...
17. One of the best things you've done for me lately is...
18. A way I think we're very similar is...
19. A way I think we're different is...
20. Ways that I sometimes make our relationship difficult are...
21. Ways that you sometimes make our relationship difficult are...
22. One way that you can improve our relationship is...
23. One way I can improve our relationship is...
24. FOR TEEN: Something I've always wondered about our family is...
    FOR DAD: Something about my family life I enjoyed growing up and something that was challenging...
25. A subject I find difficult to talk about with you is...
26. A subject I think you find difficult to talk about with me is...
27. An apology I've wanted to make to you is...
28. One of my greatest fears is...
29. I think one of your greatest fears is...
30. Something I need more of (e.g., time, help, respect) from you is...
31. Something I think you need more of from me is...
32. If today was our last day together, one thing I would want to make sure you know is...
33. In the next six months, I want us to...

The Third Practice: Connecting Emotionally

End of Practice Commitments

Based on what you've learned in The Third Practice, consider making 2 to 3 commitments to yourself, your children or any other important people in your life. Write in as little or as much detail as necessary:

1

2

3

The Fourth Practice
Model Healthy Relationships

The ideas and actions in Reflections I and II are closely adapted, with permission, from the work of bestselling author, relationship expert, and therapist Terry Real. My adaptation is a primer to what is a larger body of work found in his latest book, "The New Rules of Marriage: A Breakthrough Program for 21st Century Relationships." I have included specific references for further reading on each concept and skill. Having worked closely with Terry at his Relational Life Institute, I highly recommend his books and programs for couples. To learn more, visit relationallifeinstitute.com

While the first three practices centered mostly on your role as a dad, the fourth practice begins with a focus on your adult relationships. Whether or not you are currently with your child's mother, or even in a relationship at all, does not matter; Reflections I and II are intended to give you insight into your own behavior as well as a practical approach to being skillful in your many adult relationships (e.g., at work, with friends, with your child's mother). Reflection III asks you to apply what you've learned in this practice to raising healthy sons and daughters.

The author James Baldwin once said, "Children have never been very good at listening to their elders, but they have never failed to imitate them."

The author and activist James Baldwin once said, "Children have never been very good at listening to their elders, but they have never failed to imitate them." Just as you have probably adopted some of the characteristics of your own parents, your children will likely imitate you as well. Specifically, how you behave in relationships at home becomes a blueprint for your children to follow, for better and for worse. How you treat your children's mother is perhaps the most important of all; recent research found that the most important factor in helping children become healthy, happy adults, was the quality of the relationship between their parents.[14]

In this practice you will be introduced to Terry Real's Relationship Empowerment Model.™[15] It is based on the idea that a relationship is not something you have, it's something you do.

more >

Getting physically fit requires going to the gym regularly and becoming more health conscious in general. Being healthier in your relationships isn't much different: you learn skills to practice and develop an awareness of how you think, feel, and act in any given situation. This awareness is called a second consciousness.[16]

In a relationship, your first consciousness is your usual, habitual, knee-jerk reaction. For example, I walk in late from work and my wife greets me with a list of things I forgot or neglected to do that day. My first consciousness is a gut response, the part of me that feels criticized and therefore justified in retaliating with, "Who do you think you are talking to me that way. Do you know what it's like to come home from a long day and... (blah, blah, blah)." Again, that is my knee-jerk reaction. Second consciousness is the more skilled and mature part of me that knows better. On a good day, it's a voice in my head that says, "Stop and take a breath. Don't say a word. Don't even open your mouth. Just cool down first." When every bone in my body wants to shout back, second consciousness is the reminder that I have a choice to act differently.

Reflection I focuses on what Real calls *The Five Losing Strategies*™ in relationships, those knee-jerk responses - such as the example of 'retaliating' given above - that always lead to more trouble. By understanding your own losing strategies and how they are learned in your family of origin, you will begin to see more clearly the places you get stuck in relationships.

Conflict is part of any relationship. In a healthy relationship, however, that conflict gets handled or managed, not avoided. When a couple constantly fights, their conflict affects their child's schoolwork and ability to form friendships and even makes the child more susceptible to illness.[17] Reflection II introduces you to a step-by-step approach for handling conflict called the Repair Process.™ Also, practical suggestions for how to cherish and appreciate the positive aspects of a relationship are given.

The end of this practice, Reflection III, returns to your role as a dad. To truly develop healthy relationships and raise our sons and daughters to be happy and whole requires us to redefine manhood. After reflecting on your own ideas about 'what it means to be a man,' you will be prompted to talk about gender stereotypes with your children. Specific suggestions for raising boys and girls today are also presented. The practice ends by asking you to challenge a common stereotype - 'go it alone' - and think about what support you'll need to continue the work you've started in this Handbook.

Reflection I

Understanding Where You Get Stuck

For many of us, just taking time to think about relationships, let alone practicing new skills, goes against what we learned about masculinity. Instead of 'doing what comes naturally,' relying on your instincts, or leaving your partner to deal with all that 'relationship stuff,' the following actions will ask you to be proactive. By stepping back, looking honestly at yourself and how you interact with others, you will develop or cultivate what is perhaps the most important skill of all: self-awareness.

Yet, no matter how self-aware or well-intentioned you are, it is a virtual certainty that things won't always go your way. The difference between a healthy and unhealthy relationship is all about what you do in those moments. Terry Real calls this the *Crunch* - the raw experience of your unmet needs.[18] Your partner criticizes you for being selfish, *Crunch*, what do you do? Or, you come home from work tired, but your partner wants to 'have a talk': *Crunch*, what do you do? Or, on a larger scale, you come to the realization that your partner is not as appreciative and understanding as you once thought: *Crunch*, what do you do?

On a good day, we might handle the *Crunch* skillfully and with a level head. However, on a bad day, most of us give up and resort to using one or more of *The Five Losing Strategies*: being right, control, unbridled self-expression, retaliation and withdrawal. These very common behaviors may seem understandable in the moment, but will guarantee failure every time. Typically, your losing strategy will trigger or reinforce your partner's losing strategy. This results in a vicious cycle called The More, The More:[19] "The more she tries to get him to talk (control), the more he avoids her (withdrawal). The more he withdraws, the more she tries to control..." and so on. The first step in breaking these cycles or 'ongoing battles' is acknowledging that the only person you can change in a relationship is yourself. Understanding your own losing strategies and where they come from is the next step.

Losing strategies are learned in childhood. The unhealthy ways you were related to as a child become 'the baggage' you carry into your relationships as an adult. If, for example, you grew up with a father who avoided conflict by going silent, withdrawal is likely one of your losing strategies today. However, as adults we often confuse our own losing strategies with normal behavior simply because they look just like 'the norms' we grew up with. Retaliation, for example, may not seem like a losing strategy to someone who grew up with an angry, explosive parent.

The good news is that losing strategies are not hard-wired. With work, they can be interrupted, managed and even stopped for good. However, it requires an honest look in the mirror and above all, a commitment to taking responsibility for our own behavior in relationships. For some men, this means letting go of the fantasy that all our relationship troubles would disappear if we just found "the right person." The following actions will help you to identify and understand the places you get stuck. In Reflection II you'll learn the skills to do something about it.

ACTION #1
Assess Yourself in Five Key Areas of Relationships

This action is intended to help you see your strengths and challenges in five key areas of relationships.* Think about your intimate relationships, either past or present, and then rate yourself using the following scale:

★☆☆ TOTAL MESS

★★☆ NEED WORK

★★★ SOLID

* For another assessment see Terry Real's *Intimacy Inventory*, pg. 26 of *The New Rules of Marriage.*

1) Speaking Up
I express a range of emotion without overwhelming others, talk about my needs and deal with others' feelings respectfully.

 2) Showing Up
I make time for my relationship, initiate and share in activities, and respond to my partner's requests for time with me.

 3) Listening
I take in what others say in a way that helps them to feel heard and not judged.

 4) Handling Conflict
I handle conflict in a direct and respectful way without intimidating, acting like a victim, or withdrawing.

 5) Getting Support
I reach out to others (friends, community, professionals) when I'm having difficulty in my relationships.

ACTION #2
Get a Reality Check

In order to have some accountability and support in doing The 5 Keys, it's important to have a witness. Find someone close to you (another dad, a friend, your partner) to discuss your assessment. Briefly explain the Handbook and this particular action. Next, read through your responses to The 5 Keys, making sure to give a reason for the ratings you gave yourself. Finally, ask your witness to say whether they agree or disagree. Take in their comments as 'food for thought' and thank them for being a witness.

WHO:
I plan to talk to

WHEN:
I will talk to them

ACTION #3
Learn The Five Losing Strategies™ in Relationships

The Five Losing Strategies are common, yet ineffective ways of trying to get your needs met in a relationship. However, it's safe to say that everyone will attempt at least one of these strategies at some point during the course of a relationship.

Please review The Five Losing Strategies.[20] At the end of each losing strategy, write down an example of when you used it or saw someone else using it. Give a few details about the situation, reactions, etc.

1. Needing To Be Right

As Terry Real says, "You can be right or you can be married. What's more important to you?" In any relationship, there are two points of view. To insist that yours is more valid, accurate or right will only lead to more conflict, not a solution.

Example: Carl is driving aggressively on the highway. His wife gets angry, says he's endangering them and tells him to slow down (this moment is the Crunch). He responds by telling her that he's not being unsafe, just aggressive. She says unsafe, he says aggressive. Unsafe. Aggressive... and on it goes.

So, who's right and who's wrong? It doesn't matter. What should matter to Carl is that his wife is uncomfortable with his driving - whether it was aggressive or unsafe. His choice is clear: insist on being right, continue driving that way and deal with the consequences of having an unhappy wife OR understand how crazy it makes her and slow down. Many guys would call that 'giving in.' Maybe it is. Always remember to ask yourself: what's more important, being right or finding a solution?

A time when I used or saw someone use this losing strategy:

_____

_____

_____

_____

2. Controlling Your Partner

For many of us, this is the most seductive of the losing strategies. Control is about trying to "get" someone to behave as we think they should. Control can be direct, such as telling someone what to do or how they feel. Or, it can be indirect, such as manipulating or emotionally blackmailing someone. It is a losing strategy for the simple reason that payback is inevitable. In a relationship, the only person you can control is yourself.

Examples of Direct Control: "Stop telling me what to do!" "You need to start being more honest with me" or "Don't get all upset and sad about it." Examples of Indirect Control: "If you really loved me then you would..." or "I wouldn't be so upset if you would stop..."

A time when I used or saw someone use this losing strategy:

_____

_____

_____

_____

_____

3. Unbridled Self-Expression

Terry Real calls this 'the barf-bag approach to intimacy.' It's based on the crazy idea that venting or spontaneously expressing everything on your mind will somehow bring you closer to your partner. Many delude themselves into thinking they're 'just being honest' when really they're just trying to make themselves feel better. Unbridled self-expression will usually leave your partner feeling helpless and angry; thoughtfully saying what's on your mind and what you need from your partner will more likely lead to solutions.

Examples: "Do you have any idea how terrible you make me feel when you..." or "I need to vent! Let me tell you exactly what it's like living with somebody like you..." or "I just want to be honest and tell you that I've been fantasizing about your best friend all weekend."

A time when I used or saw someone use this losing strategy:

_____

_____

_____

_____

4. Retaliation

Direct retaliation is essentially 'eye for an eye' behavior; we feel hurt or wronged by another person and thereby completely justified in striking back. Terry Real calls this dynamic "offending from the victim position." The impulse can be so strong that some men strike back physically, but most lash out verbally. Humiliation, ridicule, name-calling, control, and explosive anger are all forms of direct retaliation. Indirect retaliation, otherwise known as being passive-aggressive, is a way of expressing anger through withholding. It's all about what you *don't say*. Direct and indirect retaliation may feel good in the moment, as if some kind of justice was served, but they will ultimately poison a relationship.

Examples of Direct Retaliation: "Oh, so it was my fault the baby fell off the chair? Well, I didn't see you getting up and doing anything about it" or "If you're going to talk to me that way, then don't be surprised when I shout back at you." Examples of Indirect Retaliation: "No, I'm not upset, I just forgot to kiss you goodbye for the last three mornings in a row."

A time when I used or saw someone use this losing strategy:

_____

_____

_____

_____

_____

5. Withdrawal

As with retaliation and control, withdrawal can be large or very small. It can be as dramatic as storming out after an argument or as quiet as gradually holding back affection. You can withdraw from an entire relationship by leaving or by leading increasingly separate lives. Or you can withdraw from specific aspects of the relationship, such as emotionally or physically shutting down. Withdrawal is often motivated by a dislike for retaliation, an unwillingness to be vulnerable, a sense of hopelessness or just plain tiredness. You cannot get your needs met in a relationship by withdrawing them.

Examples of Big Withdrawal: Leaving entirely, not showing up, or storming out. Examples of Small Withdrawal: Refusing to discuss a certain issue because "you know" in advance it "won't get anywhere." One may withdraw affection, sex, shared activities, compliments, etc.

A time when I used or saw someone use this losing strategy:

_____

_____

_____

_____

ACTION #4
Express Anger Responsibly

Note: Action #4 is in no way a substitute for professional help. There will be cases in which skill-building activities like this will not be enough to change violent behaviors like anger, control or coercion; in these cases professional help may be needed. For a list of resources visit www. mrcforchange.org. Thanks to Juan Carlos Arean of the Family Violence Prevention Fund for providing important information for this action.

Expressing anger, even intense anger, in a relationship is not necessarily unhealthy. The critical question is how that anger is expressed: responsibly/non-violently or abusively (verbally or physically)? If a dad says to his daughter, for example, "I get really, really angry when you don't clean up your mess!" he is expressing his anger responsibly.

Responsible expressions of anger include:

- Taking full ownership of your feelings by using an "I" statement ("I am so angry").
- Resisting the urge to direct your anger *at* someone else or blame *them* for how *you* feel. Remove the phrase "you make me" from your vocabulary because it implies that you are a victim, that you simply have no control over your feelings. Instead use the phrase, "When you do ____, I feel ____."

Now, imagine the dad had said, "You're lazy! What do I look like, your maid?" Calling her a name in retaliation for her not listening crosses the line from responsible to verbally abusive.

Verbally/physically abusive expressions of anger* include:

- Control, retaliation, punishing withdrawal.
- Explicit or non-verbal threats, such as slamming doors, pounding a table, throwing things, getting in someone's face.
- Hitting, grabbing or pushing someone.
- Yelling, screaming, name calling.
- Shaming (ridicule, sarcasm) or humiliating someone.
- Telling an adult what he/she should do, think or feel.

Verbally and physically abusive expressions of anger directed at your child or done in their presence damage their self-worth and teach them to repeat the same behaviors as they grow up. Recent studies found that witnessing abuse in the home can negatively affect a child just as much as if they are abused directly.[21]

Chances are you've done one or more of these behaviors at some point. What's important to realize is that you don't need to do any of these behaviors going forward. I sometimes hear men defensively say things like, "I lose my temper, but not very often." It is NEVER OK to verbally abuse a child or partner. No matter how infrequent, these behaviors must be stopped. On the following two pages are two concrete ways you can start honoring a commitment to stop these behaviors right now.

*Abusive behavior is not always the result of misdirected anger. Often, it is due to the abusive person's desire to use coercive control against their intimate partners, children and others. In such cases, it is essential that the abusive person seek professional help, preferably by certified batterers intervention programs. To find a certified program, call your local domestic violence provider.

1. Take an adult time-out[22]

SET IT UP: Discuss with your partner or child your commitment to stopping your irresponsible anger. Let them know that if you feel like you're going to lose control of your anger, you will remove yourself to cool down (or find a distraction until cooled down). Make sure they understand and agree.

> Explaining an adult time-out to a child: *Using a time-out models how to deal with a problem, it doesn't undermine your authority. Make sure they know you won't physically leave them alone, rather you may go in another room to take a breath, count to five and return.*

STAY SELF-AWARE: Know the situations in which you are more likely to be at risk of losing your cool - when plans change abruptly, when you feel embarrassed, or during stressful times at work. Also, pay attention to your body's signals, such as sweating, changes in breathing, a feeling in your gut, etc.

LEAVING: Give a time-out signal and remove yourself. Whether you take a drive, go for a walk, or step into another room to breath or distract yourself, what matters most is that you get out of the situation. Even if your partner protests, leave anyway; you have an agreement. The alternative is to stay and risk losing it.

RETURNING: When taking a time-out, you must check-in with your partner. Terry Real recommends checking in (by phone if necessary) after 20 minutes. If more time is needed, the time between check-ins gets longer: one hour, half day, full day. When you return, do not discuss the issue for at least 24 hours. Seek help if a time-out is needed every time for the same issue.

2. The Dead-Stop Contract[23]

The time-out is of little use if YOU cannot be relied upon to interrupt your own anger or rage. Another effective intervention to try is called The Dead-Stop Contract. Here's how it works:

DISCUSS: First, and most importantly, you have to understand that your anger is a problem and be committed to stopping it. Discuss this commitment with your partner.

AGREE: Next, agree to give your partner full permission to signal you (with a hand gesture, word or phrase) when *they* think *you* are getting out of control and need a time-out. Part of this agreement is that when you see or hear the signal, you don't get to argue or even say a word; whatever you're doing or saying in the moment must come to a dead-stop. Then, take a time-out.

DEBRIEF: After a Dead-Stop Contract is used, it's best not to debrief or discuss what happened for at least a few hours.* The debrief will allow you to better understand how your behavior (whether you were getting angry or not) impacts your partner. Your job is to listen without getting defensive and try to see through your partner's eyes: "So, when I let out a big sigh and didn't say anything, you thought I was about to blow-up?" By taking their concerns seriously and making necessary changes, you can bring safety back into the relationship.

As with the time-out, if after a few hours you still cannot discuss the situation without arguing or getting worked up again, seek outside help.

ACTION #5
Understand the Childhood Roots of Adult Relationships

Our template or blueprint for how to behave in relationships is largely a result of what we saw and experienced in our home growing up.[24] Similarly, the losing strategies we tend to use today are usually strikingly similar to those used by the adults (male and/or female) who took care of us as children. Because those losing strategies were 'the norms' we grew up with, it's often difficult for us to see when we're using them as adults.

For example - When my wife got angry at me for not finishing painting our kitchen, my losing strategy was to retaliate; I immediately felt attacked, became defensive, and then tried turning it around by saying that SHE was demanding too much of me. In short, my argument was 'It's your fault I didn't finish because you expect too much of me.' In the moment, I seemed to have 'forgotten' that I was the one who'd agreed to finish the job by that point.

Growing up, I can't count the number of times I watched my father claim to be a victim of my mother's 'demands' and then, feeling hurt, justify his own angry response. While I'm not nearly as volatile as my father, it's no coincidence that our characteristic losing strategy of direct retaliation (offending from the victim position) is very similar. Retaliation was 'the norm' I grew up with.

Think of 3 different losing strategies your mother, father or primary caregiver used with you or each other. Write down a few details about each situation.

The losing strategy my parent
(primary caregiver) used was: _____

Describe:

The losing strategy my parent
(primary caregiver) used was: _____

Describe:

The losing strategy my parent
(primary caregiver) used was: _____

Describe:

ACTION #6
Write Your Losing Strategy Profile

Take a few moments to think about which losing strategy or combination you use the most. Recall what your behavior looks like on a bad day. Or, put differently, think about yourself when you are at your worst.

It may be one strategy, such as control, or a two-step, such as 'first I try to *be right* and when that doesn't succeed I *withdraw* bitterly.' Don't get picky, just try and get a flavor for your characteristic responses to conflict, big or small. Also, consider what you learned from your parents/caregivers growing up.

If you are really having trouble with this, simply explain the idea to your partner or someone who knows you well and see if they can help you with your losing strategy profile.[25]

The losing strategy, or combination of strategies,
I use most often are:

ACTION #7
Stop those
"Arguments that never end"

Most couples tend to have an argument or conflict that happens over and over, no matter how the situation may change. Terry Real calls this "a couple's bad deal."[26] How it works: one person's losing strategy triggers the other's losing strategy. Then, the losing strategies intensify and begin to reinforce each other.

A powerful tool for identifying your own 'bad deal' is to use the phrase The More/The More.

The more I do   _losing strategy x_
the more my partner does   _losing strategy y_

The more my partner does   _losing strategy y_
the more I do   _losing strategy x_

1. **Review the following three examples of The More/The More**

    The more he gets defensive (being right)
    The more his partner complains (retaliation, passive)
    The more his partner complains
    The more he gets defensive.

    The more his partner interrogates him (control)
    The more he lies (passive retaliation)
    The more he lies
    The more his partner interrogates him.

    The more his partner criticizes him (unbridled self-expression)
    The more he avoids his partner (withdrawal)
    The more he avoids his partner
    The more his partner criticizes him.

2. Write about your experience of "the more"

Think about the common, reoccurring arguments you have
(or had) with your partner. What are the losing strategies (or
combination of losing strategies) each of you tends to use?
Write about two different possibilities for The More/The More?

1)   The more I _____

         losing strategy is: _____

The more my partner _____

         losing strategy is: _____

The more my partner _____

            The more I _____

2)   The more I _____

         losing strategy is: _____

The more my partner _____

         losing strategy is: _____

The more my partner _____

            The more I _____

3. Beginning to step out of your "bad deal"

Awareness is the first step to ending your "bad deal."

- Identify your losing strategies and where they come from (which you've done in the last two actions).

- Pay attention to when you feel stuck in The More/The More.

- Remember, the only person you can change and control in a relationship is yourself. Don't try and explain what *you* think your partner's losing strategies are.

- Interrupt your side of The More/The More: when you recognize your characteristic losing strategy taking over (i.e. you start trying to control your partner by telling them what they should or shouldn't feel), take a breath and do something different. You may ask for a time-out, apologize to your partner, or ask your partner how you could be more helpful. Don't describe what *you* think is their part of The More/The More.

With the awareness you now have, in Reflection II you will learn to step out of your bad deal altogether.

Reflection II

The Repair Process:™
Speaking and Listening

Many men get into relationship trouble for the simple reason that they stop being proactive. There's a fine line between routine and rut. Even when things appear to be running smoothly, it's important to initiate spending time together and stay tuned in to each other's daily lives. Similarly, when conflicts arise, instead of denying they exist or hoping time will heal all wounds, having a way to actively work through problems is essential.

In the first action, you will learn a simple yet powerful skill to help you take a more proactive approach to getting what you want in your relationships. Practicing this skill - what Real calls "moving from complaint to request" - will prevent resentment from building and keep your relationship on track, moving forward.[27]

However, as in all relationships, inevitably you or your partner will hit the Crunch - feeling deeply hurt, angry, or disappointed - and fall off the track completely. Whether it's about one person feeling unappreciated or the other's drinking problem, in moments like these every couple needs a way to fix the damage.

The most common approach couples use to solving problems or issues is to have a dialogue: you tell me your side, I'll tell you mine and then we'll sort it out. For some couples this works fine. However, for many people what may start as dialogue often becomes a tit-for-tat. Whether a solution is found or one 'side' gives up, rarely do both feel truly understood.

In Actions 2 through 4 you will learn a different approach to solving problems called the Repair Process - one speaker, one listener working together on one issue at a time. In short, the speaker describes his version of the issue and says what he needs from the listener in order to repair it. The listener does everything possible to understand the speaker's perspective, acknowledge their contributions to the issue and give the speaker whatever's needed to fix it.

ACTION #1
Shift from Complaint to Request

Real describes this skill as "taking a more assertive, less passive and reactive approach to getting your needs met in a relationship." Instead of criticizing your partner for what they did wrong, tell them what right would look like. The shift is from a past-negative focus to a positive-future focus.[28] As you read the following examples, think about which is more likely to result in a fight and which you would rather hear:

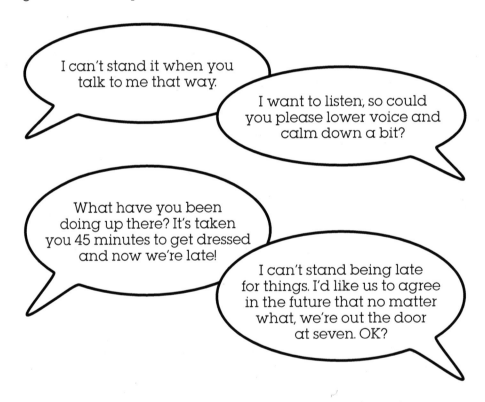

I can't stand it when you talk to me that way.

I want to listen, so could you please lower voice and calm down a bit?

What have you been doing up there? It's taken you 45 minutes to get dressed and now we're late!

I can't stand being late for things. I'd like us to agree in the future that no matter what, we're out the door at seven. OK?

When faced with a relationship problem, many of us find complaining (unbridled self-expression), arguing (being right) or staying silent (withdrawing) is easier than respectfully and specifically asking for what we need from our partner. It's also safer because never asking means you can't be disappointed or let down.

A friend of mine, for example, complained that his wife regularly rejected his attempts to initiate sex. Months of arguing got him nowhere. Finally, he stopped complaining and requested two things: first, a discussion about what he could do to improve their sex life and secondly, an agreement that one night each week they would be 'physically intimate.' Feeling empowered by his requests, and no longer criticized, his wife responded positively.

If you want something to change in your relationship, you have to ask for it; arguing, complaining or saying nothing renders your partner helpless. A specific request enables them to deliver for you.

Catch Yourself Complaining and Shift to Request

The next time your partner pushes your buttons, before you speak, ask yourself these two questions:[29]

1. **What do I want here? What's my goal?**

2. **Is what I'm about to say going to lead me closer or further away from my goal?**

If you realize that what you're about to say will be unconstructive (one of The Five Losing Strategies), then don't say it. Unless, of course, your goal is to 'vent' or 'be heard,' which almost guarantees a fight. If, on the other hand, your goal is to have a different outcome in the future, it's in your best interest to request what you'd like to see happen.

Over the next week, write briefly about 3 situations in which you catch yourself complaining (or saying something unconstructive) but manage to shift to request.

Complaint   Request

1.

2.

3.

ACTION #2
Use the Repair Process to Speak Skillfully and Respond Generously

Bringing up a problem or an issue you have with your partner is never easy. In this action you will be introduced to the Repair Process, a simple, structured way for you and your partner to deal with difficult situations. The Repair Process is comprised of two basic components: speaking skillfully* and responding with generosity. These two valuable skills, when put to use in the Repair Process, will enable you and your partner to address issues with respect and resolve them with compassion.

First, learning to speak with skill will insure that you take full responsibility for yourself (instead of blaming your partner), stay focused on a particular incident and specific behaviors, and offer your partner concrete ways to make you feel better.

Next, you will also be introduced to the other side of the equation - how to respond with generosity. As with speaking, the challenge is to respond in a way that makes matters better, not worse. Real says, "Remember, an unhappy or upset partner is primarily interested in only one thing: whether or not you care. Responding by explaining yourself, sharing your opinion of what's going on, or rebutting a claim they make will convince your partner that the only person you care about is yourself." The best response is to place yourself fully in the service of your partner. This requires restraint and an attitude of generosity.

* *Based on the Feedback Wheel initially created by Janet Hurley, modified by Terry Real.*

This action plays out in three steps:

1. **Speaking With Skill.**
   In this step you'll learn the five basic steps to building a straightforward, honest approach to problem-solving.

2. **Responding with Generosity.**
   In this next step you'll learn how to "listen to understand." This skill is about empathy and giving.

3. **Practice the Repair Process**
   After you have a chance to review the Repair Process, you will be asked to practice using it with your partner (or close friend), using a small but real issue from your lives. It's important that you pay attention to both the speaking and responding sections. After you have done it once, the speaker and responder should switch roles and begin the process again.

1. Speaking With Skill

Speaking with skill (Terry Real calls this Speaking Out with Love and Savvy) consists of five steps. Each of the steps should be only one or two sentences long. Stick to the language, even if sounds formal or awkward.

1 Reporting what you saw & heard | "When you..."

Just the facts, no interpretation. As specifically and concretely as you can, say what behaviors troubled you. What you describe should be something a video camera could record. If it couldn't be recorded on video, you've probably started interpreting your partner's attitude, motivations, or emotional state. If you say, "you acted like a jerk," your partner may not agree. Whereas if you say "you kept sighing and shaking your head" there is little to argue about. If you want your partner to fix or do something differently, they need to understand exactly what you're talking about.

NOT SPECIFIC	SPECIFIC
"When you left in a rage."	"When you slammed the door."
"When you were rude."	"When you interrupted me."
"When you take your stress out on us."	"When you shouted at the kids."

2 Saying what you think | "What I imagined was..."

In this step, you say what your partner's behaviors (from step one) meant to you. Despite sounding awkward, the phrase "what I imagined" clearly establishes that this is *your* story, not *the* story. For example, a wife said to her husband, "When you yelled at the waitress, I imagined you were being rude." He responded by saying, "I was being assertive, not rude." What's important is not *who is right* but that she experienced his behavior as rude.

3 Stating your emotions | "About that I feel..."

As simply as possible, identify and name the feeling(s) you experienced during this incident. A common mistake is to confuse feelings with beliefs. "I feel like you don't respect me" or "I feel like it's not important to you" are not feelings. When you say "I feel" it should be followed by one word: angry, disappointed, worried, etc. Keep it simple. As men, many of us tend to lump our feelings into one - anger. I encourage you to express other feelings that often underlie anger, such as hurt, fear or shame.

4 Asking for repair | "What I would like is..."

In this step, you tell your partner how they can help you feel better. Like step one, this step is all about being specific and concrete. You can request that your partner change an attitude, behave differently or even "get" something; you must, however, explain precisely what your partner can do or say to demonstrate those changes. Say, for example, that you would like your partner to change their attitude toward money and spend less freely. To make this specific you could ask them to start doing the family budget. Requests that are too vague, such as "Stop being so critical," or utterly unrealistic, like "Never be late again," set both of you up for failure. Ask for what you need and what you believe your partner can reasonably deliver. You may get some, none or all of what you asked for. Or, your partner may have questions, want to negotiate, or try and argue with you. Assure your partner that you will gladly listen to any feedback they have for you, but now you would like to hear their response.

5 Help your partner deliver | "What can I do..."

You, the speaker, are now at the service of the responder. After your partner has agreed to give you what they can, thank them and ask the following question: "What can *I do* to help *you* deliver on *your* commitment?" Terry Real refers to this as the "Golden Rule for Relationship."[30] For example, if you requested more physical affection, your partner may respond with, "If you gave me a quick reminder, that would help. You could also pay more attention to me and the kids." It's in your best interest to do everything you possibly can to help your partner deliver on your request.

SOME EXAMPLES

When you said I wasn't prepared for the trip and told me what to do,
What I imagined was that you don't trust my judgment & need to be in control.
About that I feel angry, a little sad and worried.
What I would like is to feel more trusted. If you could tell me that you are feeling anxious instead of telling me what to do, that would help a great deal.

When you called me selfish in front of the kids,
What I imagined was that you want them to think I'm not a good person.
About that I feel ashamed and upset.
What I would like is for you to tell me specifically what's bothering you and how I could change it, and not do it in front of the kids.

2. Responding With Generosity

In the first three steps of your response the focus should be on what Real calls Listening To Understand."[31] YOU SHOULD *SAY* VERY LITTLE. Be as empathetic as possible. Try and see the situation through their eyes. You can't fix anything for your upset partner unless you listen enough to know what's wrong. Focus on your partner's needs, not your own. Steps four and five are more about acknowledging your role in the problem and doing your best to give your partner what they are asking for.

1   Understand your partner's issue | Respond to "When you…"
The most important thing to remember is that your partner may have a completely different version of how things went on a particular occasion. Rather than trying to convince them that your version is right, try to understand theirs. If there is something you just don't understand, asking your partner a clarifying question is reasonable. However, make sure any questions you ask are truly in the spirit of understanding your partner, not to prove them wrong.

2   Walk in your partner's shoes | Respond to "What I imagined was…"
To walk in your partner's shoes, you must step out of your own. Try to understand the connection between their version of what happened and the meaning they gave those events. Then, reflect it back to them. For example, you may say, "So, when I came home late again, you imagined I had a problem with working too much and that I didn't care about the family. Do I have that right?" Rather than thinking that your partner must be crazy, be curious and try to follow their logic. If you can see through their eyes, you may understand how their story makes perfect sense to them.

3   Validate your partner's emotions | Respond to "About that I feel…"
Once you understand your partner's story - what they imagined (step two) about the initial events (step one) - it will be much easier to empathize with their feelings. If, for example, your partner said, "When you didn't answer me, I imagined you were ignoring me…" it's easy to understand how they may feel angry or hurt (even if you weren't trying to ignore them). How one *thinks* about a situation will determine how they *feel* about it. In this step, simply validate your partner's feelings while putting your own aside.

4 **Clarify/Acknowledge/Give** | Respond to "What I would like is…"
Once your partner feels satisfied that you 'get' what they're saying, it's time to **clarify** exactly what their request is: "You want me to be home for dinner at least three nights each week. Is that right?" Once you're certain about what's being asked of you, the real challenges of repair begin: taking responsibility and taking action. Instead of defending yourself, **acknowledge** any contribution you made to the issue (i.e., "I realize that I get home late a lot" or "I did raise my voice"). This will reassure your partner that you are accountable for your actions. At the very least, acknowledge your partner's point of view, "I can understand how you would see it that way." Finally, **give** what you can. Meet your partner's request by saying what you're *willing* to do, not what you *refuse* to do. Of course, some requests may go too far; there's nothing wrong with saying no or negotiating. Don't, however, confuse generously giving with giving in; just ask yourself, which is more important, winning or having a happy, satisfied partner?

5 **Tell the speaker how to help** | Respond to "What can I do…"
By this point, you have already agreed to meet the speaker's request as best as possible. Now, let the speaker know exactly what *they* could do to help *you* deliver on *your* commitment. For example, the speaker requested that you control your anger more around the kids and you agreed. Something the speaker could do to help you deliver (control your anger) might be to give you signal when they think you're getting angry.

3. Practice Using the Repair Process

Now that you understand the two sides to the Repair Process it's time to see how these skills work together. The idea behind practicing the Repair Process is to help you get comfortable with this new way of communicating.

1 Think about a small conflict or issue

Think about a small conflict or issue you recently had with your partner (or another important adult). Perhaps you were trying to express something and were not well received. Maybe your partner did or said something that upset you, but you didn't react well. Choose something small, not a major conflict. It may help to write down what happened and what was said.

2 Imagine you could do it over again

Next, imagine you could go back and do this conflict over again. Using the Repair Process Worksheet on the following pages, write down what you would say in the Speaker boxes. Don't write anything in the Responder boxes.

3 Ask your partner to participate

Now, ask your partner if they would be willing to participate in an activity with you. Tell them you are practicing a new skill designed to help you be a better partner. Explain that you want to recreate one of your conflicts and do it over using this new skill. If they agree, your partner should read over the entire Repair Process. Discuss anything they don't understand together.

4 Do all five steps of the Repair Process

Finally, do the five steps of the Repair Process. You will speak first. When finished, ask your partner if they would like to have a turn as speaker. If so, go back through the Repair Process. If not, thank your partner for participating. Make sure to discuss what each of you experienced during this action.

The Repair Process Worksheet

Copy these two pages so that both you and your partner can take simple notes on what you want to say and follow the Repair Process.

Speaker   ## Responder

1	**Report what you saw & heard** Remember, be specific about your issue or problem, just the facts. **When you...**	**Listen to understand** Focus on *their* version of what happened. *Speak very little.*

2	**Say what you think** How you feel about what you described above. **What I imagined was...**	**Walk in speakers' shoes** Understand how their story makes sense *to them. Speak very little.*

3

State your emotions
Keep it simple. Feelings, not beliefs.

About that I feel...

Validate their emotions
Put your own emotions aside for now.
Speak very little.

4

Ask for repair
Be specific and tangible. What do you want the responder to do?

What I would like is...

Clarify/Acknowledge/Give
Summarize what you heard in steps 1 through 4. Own your part in the issue and give what you can.

5

Help your partner deliver
Ask "what can *I* do to help *you* deliver on my request?"

What can I do...

Tell speaker how to help
Let speaker know what they can do to help you deliver on your commitment.

Reflection III

Being Better Men

In the Fourth Practice you were introduced to the skills for repairing your relationship when things get tough. However, an absence of conflict doesn't necessarily make a relationship harmonious. Just 'getting along' is a recipe for boredom, not a model for healthy intimacy. Remember, a relationship is not something you *have*, it's something you *do*.

So, what can you *do*? For starters, think back to a time when you first fell deeply in love. Then, make a list of everything you did in those early stages, whether out of genuine love or simply to make a good impression - maybe you gave flowers for no particular occasion, had soul-bearing discussions, listened attentively, gave a thoughtful gift, or were generous with compliments. Then, from your list, commit to doing at least two of those actions on a regular basis. Being open, expressing appreciation, sharing the load, paying attention and taking an active interest in your partner's life are all essential components of *cherishing your relationship*.

For most of us, taking such a proactive approach to cherishing our relationship will feel unnatural or even contrived. Unfortunately, what often seems more 'natural' is to put our energy towards work, parenthood, and/or community life. By and large, most of us probably didn't grow up watching our father insist that our mother make more time for the relationship by doing 'date nights.' While historically qualities like cherishing, nurturing and caring have been labeled as "feminine," times certainly are changing. Sharing the responsibility for the health of our relationships - in good times and bad - requires nothing short of a new vision of manhood.

The final section of the Fourth Practice asks you to focus on creating that new vision. Today, our sons and daughters are constantly bombarded with messages that reinforce the worst, most stereotypical version of masculinity. For example, much of the entertainment industry - from movies to television to music - insists on marketing images of men as violent, aggressive, sexist, homophobic, or downright stupid. Even children's toys play to the same one-dimensional views of gender; it's blue or pink, guns or dolls, monster trucks or strollers. As the most important man in our children's lives, it is our job to teach them something different about men and masculinity.

If we want to raise our sons to be tough *and* tender and our daughters to be caring *and* courageous, then we must model these qualities in all of our own relationships. In the following actions, you will be asked to reflect on your own boyhood as well as discuss the gender stereotypes your sons and daughters face today. As a final action, you will brainstorm the skills and support you'll need to continue the Four Practices in the future.

ACTION #1
Raising Boys: Understand the Pressure to "Act Like a Man"

1. **Review the following activity called "Act Like a Man"**
   This activity is designed to help you understand and discuss the ways boys feel pressured (mostly by other males) to conform to unhealthy gender stereotypes. This is an adaptation of the original activity created by the Oakland Men's Project.[32]

   HOW IT WORKS:

   A. First, I ask the group of boys to describe in detail "boys or men who get respect." How do they behave and not behave? What traits or characteristics do they have? What do they wear or not wear? How do they treat girls? How do they treat other boys? I ask them to think of males at school, in the media, at home, in their community, on sports teams, etc. These responses are inside the middle box on the following page.

   B. Next, using the same questions as above, I ask them to describe "boys or men who DO NOT get respect." The responses are to the right of the box on the following page. I also ask them for examples of how "a boy without respect" might be treated verbally/physically. These responses are left of the box.

   C. As we finish filling in the box, I pose questions such as: What are the benefits of acting in ways that are in the box? Do you lose anything by staying in the box? Is there anything good about being outside the box? How does the box affect your relationships with others? How do boys try to prove they're in the box? What sustains the box? How could it be changed?

   The responses on the next page are drawn from doing this activity with various groups of boys/men in different contexts.

VERBAL ABUSE

Fag

Punk

Girl

Wimp

Pussy

PHYSICAL ABUSE

Beat Up

Pushed around

Bullied

Isolated

Hassled

Murdered

BOYS WHO GET RESPECT

Is tough/hard/strong

Is his own man/doesn't need help

Makes fun of gays/isn't girly

Stays in control/holds it together

Works a lot/gets the job done

Is a good athlete/likes sports

Isn't emotional

Has style/doesn't try too hard

Has money

Eats steak

Is cut/has muscles

Takes risks

Doesn't back down

Is a player/gets lots of girls

BOYS WHO DON'T GET RESPECT

Acts feminine/gay

Doesn't play sports

Is weak or soft

Cries/is emotional

Acts too smart

Isn't tough

Needs help

Told what to do/whipped

Can't take a joke

Is too sensitive

Acts confused

2. **Read the important lessons from the "Act Like a Man" box**
   The following points will help you understand what a powerful impact the box has on boys' lives - their relationships with girls and women, other boys and men, and to themselves. Also, these points will put this activity in a larger societal context.

   ### THE LESSONS OF "ACT LIKE A MAN"

   - Pressure to be in the box starts as early as when boys are four-years-old. The negative consequences for stepping out of the box can limit boys' behavior and expression from this young age.

   - The responses listed in the box will vary depending on factors such as the ethnicity, age, race, and/or socioeconomic background of the participants. However, responses such as 'be tough,' 'stay in control,' and 'don't show vulnerability,' are common to most groups.

   - The individual behaviors/characteristics listed in the box, such as "is tough" or "plays sports," are not bad. However, when a boy has to worry about being teased or bullied because he's not tough or isn't interested in sports, there is a problem.

   - Joking, teasing, shoving and hitting are ways boys test to see who is in the box. Not wanting to be considered outside the box, most boys become bystanders to teasing, harassment and violence.

   - For teenage boys, the following behaviors are often rewarded by establishing their place in the box: drinking excessively, experimenting with drugs, taking dangerous risks, disrespecting girls, demonstrating physical or psychological violence, being needless, playing dumb, etc.

- Boys and men often use physical or psychological violence as a way to remove doubt about their manliness. Posing as aggressive or threatening is often enough to establish oneself as in the box.

- Inside the box is the culture's dominant or 'normalized' masculinity. Stay inside and you are granted certain power and privilege. Anyone who deviates or is considered outside the box is suspected of being gay or not a 'real man' and faces the potential of being ridiculed, isolated, bullied, assaulted or worse.

- Parents may reinforce the box by *overemphasizing* sports or other traditionally male activities, withholding physical affection from boys as early as four years old, making comments like "that's for girls," or discouraging boys from behaviors, language or activities they fear others may perceive as gay or effeminate.

- Two policing mechanisms that keep boys in the box are homophobia (fear and hatred of homosexuals, fear of being perceived as homosexual) and fear of being thought of as less than a "real man." These fears keep many boys and men from speaking out against harassment of gay/lesbian/bisexual/transgendered people and the mistreatment of women.

3. **Fill in your experience with the "Act Like a Man" box**
   Think about your school years and what you learned about
   manhood. Fill in the blank box to the right.

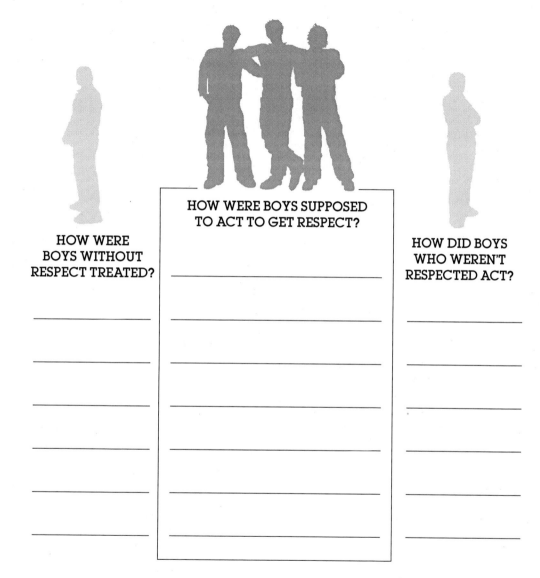

HOW WERE BOYS SUPPOSED TO ACT TO GET RESPECT?

HOW WERE BOYS WITHOUT RESPECT TREATED?

HOW DID BOYS WHO WEREN'T RESPECTED ACT?

ACTION #2
Raising Girls: Understand the Pressure to "Act Like a Lady"

This "Act Like a Lady" box is designed to help you understand and discuss the ways girls feel pressured (by each other and by males) to conform to unhealthy gender stereotypes.[33]

THE LESSONS OF 'ACT LIKE A LADY'

- Pressure to be in the box starts as early as when girls are four years old.

- The responses listed in the box will vary depending on factors like the ethnicity, age, race, or socioeconomic background of the participants. However, responses having to do with physical appearance, sexuality, caretaking and pleasing are common to most groups..

- Girls who are considered to be in the box have power and privilege. This gives incentive for girls to push each other out by gossiping, spreading rumors, giving the silent treatment and other forms of bullying and covert aggression.[34]

- The pressure on girls to conform to idealized, unrealistic images of beauty is overwhelming. A recent study found one-third of all twelve and thirteen year old girls are actively trying to lose weight by dieting, vomiting, diet pills or laxatives.[35]

- Girls face pressure from other girls to stay in the box, but they also face the very real threat of men's violence against women. Sixty percent of all rape victims are raped before the age of eighteen.[36]

- In a media culture saturated with images of women's objectified bodies, young girls get the message that their sexuality is a source of power. The sad irony is this so-called power often ends up leaving girls more subordinate and vulnerable to harassment, abuse or violence.

VERBAL ABUSE

Dyke

Whore

Fat

Slut

Bitch

PHYSICAL ABUSE

Isolated

Bullied

Assaulted

Harassed

Raped

Killed

GIRL WHO GETS RESPECT

Good listener/nice

Thin/pretty/clean

Keeps up with style/shops

Flirt/bad girl/sexy

Is desirable

Is emotional/nurturing

Is athletic

Speaks her mind

Has a "nice booty"

Has to "do it all"

Gossips

Isn't "loose" or "slutty"

Cooks/cleans

GIRL WHO DOESN'T GET RESPECT

Doesn't care about her looks

Is dirty/messy

Is too tomboy-ish

Bookish/smart

Acts slutty

Too loud

Is a real lesbian

Is too fat

No interest from boys

Has no friends

ACTION #3
Review the Three Things You Can Do to Raise Healthy Sons and Daughters

1. Be Gender Literate

If we want to raise our sons and daughters to be healthy and whole, to have a range of human qualities like strength, sensitivity, assertiveness, and caring, then we must be *literate* about the ways gender stereotypes impact their lives. As demonstrated by the box activities, both boys and girls are pressured to conform to very limited, stereotypical versions of masculinity and femininity. Some ideas for being more gender literate include:

Question your own assumptions, ideas and beliefs about gender.
What messages did you get about being a man when you were young? What did you learn about girls and women? Did you get any conflicting messages, such as "Always respect girls" and "It's acceptable to joke or comment about girls' bodies." Think about the ways you reinforce the box (stereotypical masculinity/femininity) and how you challenge it.

Challenge gender stereotypes.
Look at the different activities you encourage and don't encourage your sons and daughters to participate in, the toys you approve or disapprove of, or the behaviors you support and don't support. How, for example, would you feel about your teenage daughter wanting to work in construction or your five year-old son playing with his sister's babies? Driving past a baseball diamond recently with my two children, I said to my son, "Jake look at that!" It was as if I'd temporarily *forgotten* that my daughter loves baseball as well. The not-so-subtle message I gave her was "baseball is really for boys." This example points to the importance and difficulty of staying aware of how we shape and influence our children's lives.

Pay attention to what your children learn about gender from others.
Pay attention to the messages your sons and daughters get from
you, other family members, the media, their peers, religious or ethnic
traditions, their coaches and teachers, etc. about how they are supposed
to be, to look and to act certain ways based on being male or female.
For example, I started to pay attention to how often friends and family
members referred to my four-year-old daughter as 'pretty.' The word
seems to be like a default, as if there were no other ways to describe a
girl. From a very early age she already senses that *how she looks is very
important.* This is a message that will, as she graduates from princesses to
pop stars, likely become *how she looks is what matters most.* We cannot
intervene if we are unaware of such powerful, unhealthy messages.

For those with daughters, I encourage you to focus on her thoughts,
actions, and dreams, not her looks. Also, never make comments about her
weight. Research indicates a girl's perception of her weight and shape
during childhood is greatly influenced by her father. Dads who criticize
their daughters weight and shape can increase the risk for the eating
disorder bulimia.[37]

2. Discuss the "Act like a..." boxes with your children

If your children are younger than six, discuss with your partner, friend, etc.

Ask your son or daughter about their experience of the box.
How do boys and girls who get respect or are popular behave? Do girls feel pressured to look a certain way? Do boys try to act tough? Ask them if they've ever felt like they were outside of the box?

Tell stories about your experience of gender stereotypes and the pressure to 'act like a man' growing up.

Stories for your daughter:
> A time you felt pressured (as a boy) to behave a certain way towards girls, how you handled it and what you learned.
> A time, as a boy, you were nervous around girls.
> What it means to you today to respect girls and women.
> What you love, respect and find unique about your daughter.

Stories for your son:
> A time (as a boy) you felt pressured to take a risk in order to prove you were a 'real man.'
> Behaviors in the box that you have had to unlearn as a man or as a dad, such as 'don't ask for help' or 'don't be emotional.'
> How fear of being labeled as gay or effeminate caused you to avoid doing certain activities or expressing certain feelings growing up?
> Ways the pressure to act like a man affected your relationships with girls and other boys.

Help your children become mindful of gender stereotypes.
A dad told me a story about how his seven year-old boy wanted to wear his sister's pink sandals to school one day. His first reaction was to tell his son to change his shoes. Instead, he asked the boy questions such as "Do other kids wear these shoes?" and "What kinds of reaction

do you think others will have?" In short, he helped his son think through and make an informed decision instead of simply crushing his idea. With your children, discuss the costs and benefits of being inside and outside of the box and following gender stereotypes. Emphasize the limitations of having to conform to a stereotype. Also, acknowledge that stepping out of the box is difficult (in some cases dangerous), but ultimately important for their individuality. You should also lead by example.

Allow your children to see the many ways to be a man or woman. Introduce your son and daughter to a range of men and women in your life - friends, family members, co-workers - and have them talk about what being a man or being a woman means to them. Try to expose them to people who defy stereotypes of masculinity and femininity.

FURTHER READING AND VIEWING FOR THIS ACTION:

The Gendered Society by Michael S. Kimmel
Gender and Teaching by Janie Victoria Ward, Frances A. Maher
Reaching Up For Manhood by Geoffrey Canada
The Will To Change by bell hooks
Odd Girl Out by Rachel Simmons
Queen Bees and Wannabes by Rosalind Wiseman

Videos you can find at Mediaed.org:
Killing Us Softly 3: Advertising's Image of Women by Jean Kilbourne
Tough Guise: Violence, Media and The Crisis In Mankind by Jackson Katz
Hip Hop: Beyond Beats and Rhymes by Byron Hurt

3. Get involved. Be active.

Encourage your children's school to teach media literacy.
America is among the only countries in the developed world that does not teach children how to understand and be critical of the media they interact with on a daily basis.[38] Young girls, for example, need to know how to read fashion magazines critically so they can determine for themselves which images of women's bodies are unhealthy and unrealistic. Similarly, boys should be able to critique and discuss how they might be influenced by advertisements that equate drinking alcohol with being manly.

Recent research into children's television and popular G-rated movies found that female characters had fewer speaking parts than males and were far more likely to be in the role of caregiver. Male characters were often portrayed as dumb, funny, bad and violent (male characters of color were disproportionately portrayed as violent). They also found that heavy TV viewing predicts traditional sex-role attitudes, such as girls believing that females are less competent than males, or boys believing that household chores should fall along stereotypical lines.[39]

As parents we need to do our part by setting rules and discussing the media our children watch, play, and view. However, in this media dominated culture, we also need schools to make media literacy a priority.

Understand how homophobia hurts everyone.[40]
While social norms are changing, gay, lesbian, bisexual and transgendered (GLBT) people still suffer systematic harassment, discrimination and violence. GLBT youth have a suicide rate five times that of straight youth. In the National School Climate Survey 64% of ALL students reported that other students were called names or harassed at their school on the basis of their actual or perceived sexual orientation.[41] Homophobia is defined as: Fear of homosexuals; fear of being perceived as homosexual; fear of being homosexual. Homophobia can be expressed through prejudice, discrimination, harassment or acts of violence (known as "bashing").

The fear of being perceived as gay or lesbian affects ALL of our sons and daughters. Boys and girls (especially boys) will go to great lengths to establish their heterosexuality, including drinking excessively, getting violent, harassing or bullying others, and taking dangerous risks. Homophobia also inhibits young people's self-expression and creativity, can make forming same-sex friendships more difficult, and compromises their integrity by pressuring them to treat others badly.

As dads, we can challenge homophobia personally by speaking up when we hear homophobic comments from our children or other adults. We can refuse to participate in 'joking' about, harassing or insulting GLBT people. Finally, we can make sure our children's school has a comprehensive harassment and bullying policy, gender-based violence prevention program and a creates a supportive environment for all students.

Refuse to tolerate sexism.
As dads we have a very important role in stopping sexism in its many forms. We can all - boys and men included - lead happier more fulfilled lives by creating a more equal, safe, and supportive culture for girls and women. Even with all the gains of the last century, women still face alarming rates of men's physical and sexual violence, lack of parity in pay, a glass ceiling in the workplace, and the hyper-sexualized, stereotypical portrayals in film, television, music and advertising.

While this may seem overwhelming, we can start by refusing to tolerate or participate in sexist 'jokes,' joining progressive organizations like www.dadsanddaughters.com, speaking out against the hyper-sexualization of little girls in the media, purchasing alternative girl-friendly magazines like New Moon, making sure your children's school addresses sexual harassment in policy and program, and, most importantly, by talking with other dads (and moms) about how to overcome these challenges together.

ACTION #4
Make Men's Violence Against Girls and Women a Dad's Issue*

Our sons and daughters look to us as models for how to treat girls and women. We need to teach boys that acting like a man has nothing to do with demeaning, disrespecting or abusing girls and women. A man proves his strength by treating women with dignity and equality and does everything he can to make sure others do as well.[42]

Far too often, when a man makes a sexist joke or comments on a woman's body, other men (even if they are friends or co-workers) either join in or simply say nothing. Most men learned as boys that to speak up would result in accusations about their own sexuality or 'sensitivity.' Staying quiet was just easier.

It's precisely because of men's silence that our daughters have to learn to live with the fear of sexual assault (including abuse by other male family members) and harassment. If, on the other hand, men were to hold each other accountable for treating women respectfully, things would undoubtedly be much different.

As dads, we have a major stake in creating a safer world for our sons and daughters. By modeling and teaching the next generation of boys about the attitudes and behaviors that can lead to men's violence against women, changes are possible.

The five steps on the following page provide you with concrete actions you can take.

* This action was inspired by Jackson Katz, author of "The Macho Paradox," as well as Lonna Davis and Juan Carlos Arean at the Family Violence Prevention Fund.

1. **Understand the reality of violence against women today.**[43]
   Also realize that invariably in the following statistics is going to be a woman we love, whether that is a daughter, mother, sister or friend.

   - Nearly one-third of all women in the U.S. will experience physical or sexual abuse in her lifetime.
   - Girls of all races are equally vulnerable to violence by an intimate partner.[44]
   - A Harvard School of Public Health survey suggests that 1 in 5 high-school girls are physically or sexually abused by a dating partner.
   - Girls who are sexually assaulted almost always know the perpetrator (family member, acquaintance, partner). Strangers account for about 15%.
   - According to the Bureau of Justice Statistics, fewer than half (48%) of all rapes and sexual assaults are reported to legal authorities.

2. **Have the courage to look inward.** Question your attitudes. Don't be defensive when something you do or say ends up hurting someone. Try to understand how your attitudes and actions might perpetuate sexism and violence, and work toward changing them.

3. **Don't look the other way.** If a brother, friend, or co-worker is abusing his female partner – or is disrespectful or abusive to girls and women in general – don't ignore it. If you feel comfortable doing so, try to talk to him about it. Urge him to seek help. Or if you don't know what to do, consult your partner, a friend or a counselor. DON'T REMAIN SILENT.

4. **Approach gender violence as a MEN'S issue** involving men of all ages and socioeconomic, racial and ethnic backgrounds. View men not only as perpetrators or possible offenders, but as empowered bystanders who can confront abusive peers.

5. **Don't fund sexism.** Refuse to purchase any magazine, rent any video, subscribe to any website, or buy any music that portrays girls or women in a sexually degrading manner. Protest sexism in the media.

Steps 2 - 5 adapted from Ten Things Men Can Do by Jackson Katz, 1999.

Final Commitment

Keep It All Going
But Don't "Go It Alone"

In my early twenties I was confused about which career direction to follow. At the time, I recall feeling very envious of my best friend Jonah, who had known since a young age that he wanted to be a musician. I told him how lucky he was to have such clarity about his vision for the future. To this day, his response has stuck with me: "The difficult part about knowing what I want is that I'm painfully aware of when I'm not going after it. I feel a sense of responsibility to make my dreams a reality."

My hope is that as you finish this Handbook you will feel that same sense of responsibility towards realizing a new vision of fatherhood. As Modern Dads we have a gift that most of our fathers did not. It is the gift of knowing what a tremendous difference we can make in our children's lives. We see it in the research, we hear about it from the women in our lives, and we feel it in our hearts and bones: children need to feel close and connected, to feel at 'home' in their relationship with their father. They need a new kind of provider, a dad who not only supports them materially, but emotionally, physically and spiritually as well. This is a tall order indeed.

Realizing this vision and delivering for our children, families and the next generation of dads, requires stepping out of our fathers' footsteps and on to a new road. The road connecting our work life to our family life. Our head to our heart. Our desire to achieve with our need to just be. In short, it's the road that leads back home.

My own father was not expected to walk this road. Home, literally and figuratively, was a woman's domain. The so-called 'feminine qualities,' such as caretaking, emotionality and empathy, held little value in his world. We now know that these human qualities not only enrich our family's lives, but they also help us live longer. According to Dr. Eli Newberger, the messages boys and men get to 'go-it-alone' or 'not ask for help' are major contributing factors in why men die on average five years earlier than women.[45] In contrast, men who have intimacy and connection in their lives are actually healthier than men who do not.

Modern fatherhood is about filling up your life with healthy practices - showing up for your children and partner, learning new skills, building support networks, and measuring success by the quality and health of your relationships.

The vision is clear and the road is before us. Now, we must each take responsibility for becoming the Modern Dads our children and families need us to be.

Whether or not you continue to use the Handbook, occasionally refer back to it, or move on to the next book on your shelf, it's critical you develop some form of ongoing support. Choose one or more of the suggestions on the following page and set a realistic goal for getting the kind of support that will work best for you.

Final Commitment

1. **Male Friendships**
   Periodically get together with one of your male friends to check-in about fatherhood, relationships, work life, etc. This may require you to initiate such discussions and put your own 'stuff' out on the table, but will likely take your friendships to a deeper level. Remember, it's good for our children to see us model healthy male friendships and can also lighten the emotional load many of us place on the women in our lives.

2. **Dad's Groups/Men's Groups**
   Look for a supportive, activity-based, skills oriented or discussion-based group. Some groups are more formal, such as those done in therapeutic settings or through your religious affiliation. Others are less formal, such as a group of dads that work (or play sports) together and have dinner every three weeks to talk about fatherhood and family life. Schools are a great resource for parenting. More schools these days have father's clubs/groups. If the school does not have anything for dads, start a Modern Dads Group yourself.
   (email john@johnbadalament.com for tips on starting a Modern Dads Group)

3. **Your Partner or Like-Minded Couple**
   Commit to regular discussions with your partner or another like-minded couple about parenting, relationship issues, etc.

4. **Find a Good Therapist or Other Community Resources**
   Depending on where you live, a professional therapist is a good option for further exploring fatherhood and relationship issues. Community resources may include: religious organizations, local health centers, Boys and Girls Clubs, YMCA organizations, etc.

Who you plan to follow up with?

What's your time frame for follow-up
(weekly, monthly, biannually)?

NOTES/THOUGHTS:

_____

_____

_____

_____

_____

_____

_____

Endnotes

1. Kimmel, Michael S. Address. *Gender Equality: Not for Women Only* Int'l Women's Day Seminar. European Parliament, Brussels. 3/8/2001.

2. Hochschild, Arlie. *The Second Shift* Penguin, 2003.

3. Gottman, John, with Joan Declaire. *Raising An Emotionally Intelligent Child* Simon & Schuster, 1998.

4. U.S. Department of Labor. *The American Time Use Survey.* Bureau of Labor Statistics. 2005.

5. Real, Terry. *Relational Parenting.* Audio CD. 2005.

6. Real, Terry. *Relational Parenting.* Audio CD. 2005.

7. Nord, C.W. and West, J. *Fathers' and Mothers' Involvement in Their Children's Schools by Family Type and Resident Status.* U.S. Dept. of Education. National Center for Education Statistics. 2001.

8. Gottman, John, with Joan Declaire. *Raising An Emotionally Intelligent Child* Simon & Schuster, 1998.

9. Pruett, Kyle. *Fatherneed: Why Father Care is as Essential as Mother Care for Your Child* Broaway, 2001.

10. Pelach-Galil, Ricky. *The Re-Creation Of The Father By His Adolescent Son.* Dissertation to the Hebrew University of Jerusalem. 2003.

11. *Father-Daughter Summit.* National Center for Fathering. 2003.

12. Real, Terry. *The New Rules of Marriage.* Ballantine Books, 2007.

13. Pollack, William and Cushman, Kathleen. *Real Boys Workbook.* 2001.

14. Schleifler, H. The Family Law Commentator, 1994. The Timberlawn Psychiatric Institute of Dallas.

15. Real 16.

16. Real 65.

17. Gottman, John, with Joan Declaire. *Raising An Emotionally Intelligent Child* Simon & Schuster, 1998.

18. Real 38.

19. Real 66.

20. Real 34-60.

21. Groves, B.M. *Children Who See Too Much: Lessons from the Child Witness to Violence Proejct,* Beacon Press, 2002

22. Real 106.

23. Real 89.

24. Real 71-92.

25. Real 60.

26. Real 66.

27. Real 166.

28 Real 168.

29. Real 183.

30. Real 228.

31. Real 212-232.

32. Kivel, Paul and Creighton, Allan. *Helping Teens Stop Violence: A Practical Guide for Counselors, Educators and Parents.* 1990.

33. Kivel and Creighton. 85.

34. Simmons, Rachel. *Odd Girl Out: The Hidden Culture of Aggression in Girls.* Harcourt Books, 2002.

35. Kilbourne, Jean. *Can't Buy My Love: How Advertising Changes the Way We Think and Feel.* Free Press, 2000.

36. National Victims Center and Crime Victims Research and Treatment Center, *Rape in America: A Report to the Nation.* 1992.

37. Agras, W. Stewart M.D., Bryson, Susan M.A., M.S., Hammer, Lawrence D. M.D., and Kraemer, Helena C. Ph.d. *Childhood Risk Factors for Thin Body Preoccupation and Social Pressure to Be Thin.* Journal of the American Academy of Child & Adolescent Psychiatry. February 2007.

38. Kilbourne, Jean. *Can't Buy My Love.* Free Press, 2000.

39. Kelly, Joe & Smith, Stacy L., Ph.D. *Now You See 'Em, Now You Don't: Gender & Racial Disparity in TV for Children.* See Jane / Dads & Daughters. 2006.

40. Blumenfeld, Warren. *Homophobia: How We All Pay The Price.* 1992.

41. National School Climate Survey (NSCS). The Gay, Lesbian and Straight Education Network (GLSEN). 2005.

42. *Coaching Boys Into Men Playbook.* Family Violence Prevention Fund.

43. From Girls, Inc. www.girlsinc.com

44. Bureau of Justice Statistics. *Violence Against Women: Estimates from the Redesigned Survey.* August, 1995.

45 Newberger, Eli. *The Men They Will Become: The Nature and Nurture of Male Character.* Perseus Publishing, 1999.

Resources

BOOKS

George Abrahams & Sheila Ahlbrand | Boy V. Girl: How Gender Shapes Who We Are, What We Want, and How We Get Along

Nancy Slonim Aronie | Writing from the Heart

Roz Barnett & Caryl Rivers | Same Difference: How Gender Stereotypes Are Hurting Our Relationships, Our Children and Our Jobs

Warren Blumenfeld | Homophobia: How We All Pay the Price

Armin A. Brott | Father for Life: A Journey of Joy, Challenge, and Change

Mark Bryan | Prodigal Father: Reuniting Fathers With Their Children

Geoffrey Canada | Reaching Up for Manhood: Transforming the Lives of Boys in America

Stephanie Coontz | The Way We Never Were: American Families and the Nostalgia Trap

Ann Arnett Ferguson | Bad Boys: Public Schools in the Making of Black Masculinity

James Garbarino | Lost Boys: Why Our Sons Turn Violent and How We Can Save Them

Dr. James Gilligan | Violence: Reflections on a National Epidemic

Will Glennon | The Collected Wisdom of Fathers

Edward M. Hallowell, M.D. | The Childhood Roots of Adult Happiness: Five Steps to Help Kids Create and Sustain Lifelong Joy

bell hooks | The Will to Change: Men, Masculinities and Love

Iris Jacobs | My Sisters' Voices: Teenage Girls of Color Speak Out

Jackson Katz | The Macho Paradox, Why Some Men Hurt Women and How All Men Can Help

Joe Kelly | Dads and Daughters: How to Inspire, Understand, and Support Your Daughter

Jean Kilbourne | Can't Buy My Love: How Advertising Changes the Way We Think and Feel

Michael S. Kimmel | Manhood In America: A Cultural History | The Gendered Society

Paul Kivel | Men's Work: How to Stop the Violence that Tears Our Lives Apart

Paul Kivel and Allan Creighton | Making the Peace: A 15-session Violence Prevention Curriculum for Young People

William C. Klatte | Live-Away Dads: Staying a Part of Your Children's Lives When They Aren't a Part of Your Home

Michael Lamb | The Father's Role: Cross-Cultural Perspectives | The Role of the Father in Child Development

Bernard Lefkowitz | Our Guys

Margo Maine, Ph.D. & Craig L. Johnson | Father Hunger: Fathers, Daughters & Food

Jeffrey Marx | Season of Life: A Football Star, A Boy, A Journey To Manhood

Susan Maushart | Wifework: What Marriage Really Means to Women

Myriam Miedzian | Boys Will Be Boys: Breaking the Link Between Masculinity and Violence

Tamara Monosoff | The Mom Inventors Handbook: How to Turn Your Idea into the Next Big Thing | Secrets of Millionaire Moms

Michael J. Nakkula & Eric Toshalis | Understanding Youth: Adolescent Development for Educators

Kent Nerburn | Letters to My Son

Eli H. Newberger, M.D. | The Men They Will Become: The Nature and Nurture of Male Character

Tim O'Brien | The Things They Carried

Samuel Osherson | Finding Our Fathers: How a Man's Life is Shaped by His Relationship with His Father

Leonard Pitts, Jr. | Becoming Dad: Black Men & the Journey to Fatherhood

William Pollack | Real Boys: Rescuing Our Sons From the Myths of Boyhood

Kyle Pruett | Fatherneed: Why Father Care is as Essential as Mother Care for Your Child

BOOKS (continued)

Terrence Real | How Can I Get Through to You? : Reconnecting Men and Women | I Don't Want to Talk About It: Overcoming the Secret Legacy of Male Depression | The New Rules of Marriage: A Breakthrough Program for 21st Century Relationships

Olga Silverstein | The Courage to Raise Good Men

Rachel Simmons | Odd Girl Out: The Hidden Culture of Aggression in Girls

Eve Sullivan | Where the Heart Listens: A Handbook for Parents and Their Allies in a Global Society

Michael Thompson and Dan Kindlon | Raising Cain: Protecting the Emotional Lives of Boys

Janie Victoria Ward and Frances A. Maher | Gender and Teaching

David B. Wexler, Ph. D. | When Good Men Behave Badly: Change Your Behavior, Change Your Relationship

John Edgar Wideman | Fatheralong: A Meditation on Fathers and Sons, Race and Society

Andre C. Willis and Alvin F. Poussaint | Faith of our Fathers: African-American Men Reflect on Fatherhood

Rosalind Wiseman | Queen Bees and Wannabes: Helping Your Daughter Survive Cliques, Gossip, Boyfriends, and Other Realities of Adolescence

VIDEOS

All Men Are Sons: Exploring the Legacy of Fatherhood | John Badalament

Slim Hopes: Advertising and the Obsession with Thinness | Jean Kilbourne

Tough Guise: Violence, Media, and the Crisis in Masculinity | Jackson Katz

Hip Hop: Beyond Beats and Rhymes | Byron Hurt

WEBSITES

www.johnbadalament.com

www.relationallifeinstitute.com | Info about Terry Real's workshops.

www.newrulesofmarriage.com | Terry Real's new book.

www.dadsandaughters.org

www.gottman.com | The Gottman Institute is loaded with resources on parenting and relationships.

www.jacksonkatz.com

www.jeankilbourne.com

www.paulkivel.com

www.rachelsimmons.com

www.rosalindwiseman.com

www.mediaed.org | Resources on gender and the media. Look for work by Jackson Katz and Jean Kilbourne in particular.

www.ncoff.gse.upenn.edu | National Center on Fathers and Families

www.mensbiblio.xyonline.net | A comprehensive bibliography of writing and research on men by Michael Flood.

www.nlffi.org | National Latino Fatherhood and Family Institute

www.100blackmen.org | 100 Black Men of America, Inc.

www.mencanstoprape.org

www.nomas.org | The National Organization for Men Against Sexism

BLOGS

www.daddyfactory.com

www.rebeldad.com

www.momsrising.org

www.blogher.org

www.daddy-dialectic.blogspot.com

www.wimnonline.org

About John

John Badalament, Ed.M. is an international lecturer, Harvard-trained educator and leader in the fatherhood field. John is also the director of the acclaimed film for PBS, *All Men Are Sons: Exploring the Legacy of Fatherhood* and the upcoming *Gender Traps: How Marriage Problems Start In Kindergarten*. His work has been featured in *Men's Health*, *The Boston Globe*, and *Our Children*, the National PTA magazine. Over the last 15 years, John has worked with thousands of parents and children. He currently consults with schools, parent groups, mental health professionals, corrections facilities, companies and religious groups. John lives in the Boston area with his wife and two children.

Drawing on his work with thousands of dads across America and abroad, cutting edge research, his acclaimed documentary films, and the new Modern Dads Handbook, John lectures and runs workshops in a variety of settings, including schools, businesses, mental health organizations, corrections facilities, and religious groups. To learn more about his programs and products, or to sign-up for his newsletter Modern Dads,™ visit:

www.johnbadalament.com

Praise for John Badalament's Lectures

"John's work has the potential to start conversations between fathers and children all over this country."
—MICHAEL THOMPSON, Ph.D., author of *Raising Cain*

"John's powerful message is as vital to women as it is to men. It is no exaggeration to say that this compelling presentation could save some lives."
—DR. JEAN KILBOURNE, author of *Can't Buy My Love* and creator of the award-winning documentary *Killing Us Softly.*

"Don't miss any opportunity to hear him speak!"
—WILLIAM POLLACK, M.D., author of *Real Boys,* Professor at Harvard Medical School

"John is a wonderful speaker and captures his audience immediately. His lecture was informative and thought provoking. He spoke to us as a friend we've known for years. I left hungry for more!"
—MOTHER, King & Low-Heywood Thomas School, CT

"John is at the cutting edge of what men need to do right now for happier healthier relationships with their children. He discusses what needs to be done and then walks you through the process."
—FATHER, Francis Parker School, CA

"Rarely have I experienced a presentation that brought such an enthusiastic response from students, parents and teachers. I believe that for some of the participants, it was a life-changing experience."
—LARRY IVENS, Head of School, Cranbrook Schools, MI